The Beginner's Guide
to
Affiliate Marketing 2022

The Best Steps to Generate a Commission

and to Realize Your Financial Freedom

Table of Contents

Introduction

Welcome and thank you for choosing my book.

If you have been looking for a guide to Affiliate Marketing, it is because you probably already know that it represents one of the most important opportunities to earn money through online business. It is an extremely fascinating world, complex of course, but if done well it can give a lot of satisfaction both personally and financially. To achieve results in this area you cannot improvise and go by trial and error, you need preparation, study, appropriate technical tools, the right mindset, and a minimum budget to start. You must follow a set path but at the same time experiment, because there are no secret formulas or universal standards to apply.

The goal with which I wrote this guide is to share with you my personal experience and that of many experts in the business from which I studied and in turn learned, to explain step by step what affiliate marketing is and how it works. I want to give you a guideline to follow to help you build your own path, in order to avoid mistakes due to inexperience and above all give you a complete business model that you can apply to build your own path in the affiliate marketing industry. I will not fail to share with you some little tricks that I have learned with experience and that I think can help you, be useful and facilitate your business.

If you are reading this book, it is because you are certainly curious for more information or clarity on how this type of online business works. Maybe you are looking for an opportunity to increase your income or you simply want to change your life and that of your loved ones for the better. Maybe you've seen a video on YouTube and you're wondering: "*How does that guy earn so much money with affiliate marketing and afford such a high standard of living?* ". You've probably empathized and asked yourself, "*How can I do affiliate marketing from scratch?*" or "*How can I earn extra money online?*", "*Do I need specific technical skills?*", "*Is it a business model that everyone can do?*", "*Is it possible to earn a million dollars or more even in a single year?*" , and of course "*Is this the business I'm looking for and is it right for me?"*.

Personally, I can tell you that affiliate marketing, if done correctly, with commitment, consistency and perseverance is one of the most interesting opportunities that the internet world can give you nowadays. I have seen many people revolutionize their lives for the better and achieve really important results, even in economic terms for sure. As in all things and in all types of business, you must get involved and start a journey. To do, to try, to jump in, has always been the first step to success. If you are curious to find out more about affiliate marketing, all that is left for me to do is to wish you a good read for the next chapters, hoping that this book will help you and help you change your life for the better.

1°. Mindset: The Most Important Secret Ingredient of All

Before going into the merits of affiliate marketing I think it is right to make a premise on the mindset, because it is the key to success for any type of business. Perhaps it is the most important secret ingredient of all. Without the right mindset and the right mental approach, you will never be able to achieve important results both in affiliate marketing and in life in general. Therefore, let me share with you this topic because I believe that to be successful you need to make the right mental switch.

The mindset is the set of mental structures, beliefs, values, and lines of thought that guide the actions of each one of us. It is the mindset we adopt when dealing with a problem, devising a strategy, or simply carrying out an activity during our daily routine. In every area of life, in fact, it is essential to have the right approach to make the right choices that lead to the desired results. It is important, no matter what you are doing, not to be led by randomness or negativity. The Mindset serves to energize you and put you in a position to find all the means and tools you need to achieve your goal. Ambition, good will, and a predisposition to risk are useful and functional elements, but much more is needed. First, you need a huge dose of perseverance to pursue and achieve your goals. To be successful, this is another fundamental concept, it takes time. Immediacy in results is not an easily achievable plan, and the blind greed that often arises when hoping for a profit is harmful. All and now is a concept not applicable to most important projects; of course, you can be lucky and find the right way from the beginning, but it would be just luck. Finally, it is necessary to realize in time that those who tell you that everything will be quick and painless, are not telling you the truth. Very often to be successful and make a real profit it takes time, it takes a focused strategic process, it takes strategy, planning, and I repeat constancy and perseverance. In short it takes "head", that is, a mindset that keeps you focused on your goals. To become an entrepreneur, to do business and to do business online, regardless of whether you do Affiliate marketing, Amazon FBA, drop shipping, even before capital, skills, and time you need to have the real key to breakthrough, namely the winning mentality. This winning mentality characterizes all successful people on this planet. You do not have to, as is often mistakenly thought, have "natural talent" or an IQ above the norm. You can be the smartest people on campus, for example, but if you do not apply yourself, study consistently and do not take exams or study groups because you spend your time partying, playing video games or chasing all the pretty girls in your class you will never be a winning person, even with a remarkably high IQ because you won't get results. All talents must be constantly cultivated.

Shake off any negative mental attitude, do it as if negativity were a too heavy blanket or unpleasant dandruff, as you who read me have nothing less than others. Success is nothing but a continuous obsessive and persistent effort to achieve the goals you have set for yourself.

If you are a person who morally gets down easily, think about the fact that the biggest billionaires on this planet are none other than people who have continued to insist on pursuing their dreams, where others have simply thrown in the towel and given up. Every time they are interviewed, many of them modern self-made men, starting from scratch or from a simple garage, they just repeat, with an embarrassing simplicity: "If I made it, anyone can". Believe me that this is a constant and a common trait of all millionaires or billionaires on this planet. Perseverance.

Therefore, if it helps, from this page on think of me as your best motivator or your personal coach. I say try and try and try and give your best, because sooner or later the results will come. Never let difficulties get you down. If you fall, get back up.

I repeat the concept again, so that you can print it well in your mind or on your skin as if it were an indelible tattoo: perseverance is the strongest quality that distinguishes all successful people. Persevering is one of the most important qualities and habits you can acquire, but in addition to this and incredibly important factor, is that a strong determination allows you to develop other equally important qualities, first and foremost, self-esteem.

Believing in yourself and persevering are two mutually developing forces. The more persevering you are, the more you will believe in yourself and have empowering beliefs about your potential, the more persevering you will be. The more persevering you are despite defeats, disappointments, obstacles, and failures, the greater your strength and determination will be.

There will be people, not excluding friends or relatives who, not understanding your project, not to show their ignorance, out of envy or simply not knowing what the business model consists of, will try to make you give up doing something new. They will say phrases such as: *"Are you crazy?"*, *"Come back with your feet on the ground!"*, *"You'll see it's a scam, you'll lose all your money…"* and will not miss this: *"Keep doing your job and working in the factory your hours, at least you will have a secure salary!"* and so on. Of course, there is nothing wrong with working in a factory and earning a normal salary, let us be clear, these are life choices. However, you must be well convinced and confident that when you are directed along your path, no one can ever make you give up your goal. Of course, not having the support of friends and family does not help. Often morally having loved ones "against" you and who do not support, even perhaps mock or deride, makes it more complicated and difficult. Sometimes it is hard to see that people close to you do not believe in your dream (and consequently in you and your skills) but do not worry, you know how much you are worth and how successful your project can be. You will always be in time, once you achieve success, to change their minds.

I often like to repeat a famous saying: *"A lion never loses sleep over the opinions of a sheep"*. You must always remain focused on your goal. Many people get discouraged if they do not achieve their goals, get demoralized, get down on themselves and quit. This is the crucial point that distinguishes a loser from a winner.

Once you have established a strategy, however, you must pursue it with perseverance.

Perseverance is the strategic bridge that connects you with what you want to achieve. Nothing more, nothing less.

Do not get discouraged when it seems like the outcome is moving away from the goal. Simply adjust your strategy, figure out how to improve, persevere and continue to work rigorously. To give up at the first difficulties is the typical attitude of a loser and it is not compatible with the mentality of an entrepreneur or a winner.

About perseverance, the well-known Elon Musk, entrepreneur and founder, CEO and CTO of Space Exploration Technologies Corporation, co-founder, CEO and product architect of Tesla and co-founder and CEO of Neuralink, said: "If something is really important you should still try, even if the chances of failure are very high".

Before you give up, you need to understand whether you have done and executed – for real – all the necessary steps and met the physiological timelines. To put it in a nutshell and with an example, it is not tolerable to start a business and not consider the start-up, the timing necessary for the return on investment (called ROI).

The people we hang out with, the environment we are in, and even the books we read, all influence us in positive or negative ways. Every behavior we adopt, every sentence we utter that we believe to be ours, is part of an elaborate algorithm that our mind puts in place when we must respond to an external stimulus.

This algorithm is configured because of the information we possess and that, over time, we have voluntarily or involuntarily absorbed.

Whatever your path is, it is necessary to plan first and have a clear vision. What does that mean? By clear vision I mean the clearest possible image of you as the person you want to become. In fact, you do not just want success, you also want to be that person who has achieved success, whatever that word means to you. Or am I wrong? I do not think I am wrong. So, why is it especially important to have a clear vision? Because this vision will support you throughout the process of achieving your goal and will be, so to speak, the very cause of your success.

When this vision becomes, over time, a real "obsession" (and here by obsession I mean a constant and continuous repetition of that thought), that image of you will crystallize in your mind and will set in motion processes and mechanisms that will make you work automatically and tirelessly to achieve that result.

We must, in essence, follow our dreams and desires. We must then turn those dreams and desires into a clear vision of what we want to become.

Finally, we must make use of perseverance to pursue our goals.

In addition to perseverance and goals, of course, an action plan is essential.

If we want to achieve a particular goal, this should be regardless of whether it is an economic goal or any other nature, we must stop focusing on the goal as such and start thinking differently by thinking of that goal as a series of actions that have as a "consequence" the achievement of the goal itself.

For example, if you want to become rich, the goal should not be money but is to do something that attracts money: create, for example, a business that satisfies a need or solves a problem. The enterprise then attracts people who will bring in money.

The whole process ends with action. Often the most important thing is to do, to move. Fear of making mistakes, however, is and always will be a strong lever that prevents action. Acting for most people means getting out of their comfort zone, changing their habits, or simply getting involved in a new business or work adventure. Letting go of previous certainties and pushing oneself into something new and unknown frightens everyone and hinders ambition and the desire to do. The opposite would not be normal. However, it does not have to be a wall that stops us from going down the road we want to take.

Even the judgment of others, of one's own affections, perhaps used to a more traditional and conventional vision, can be another obstacle or barrier to overcome. But if you are determined and know what you want, then no one will stop you out there.

2°. Who are Advertisers and Publishers Partners/Affiliates?

How to Start Affiliate Marketing if you are a Publisher Partner/Affiliate from Scratch; How to Start Affiliate Marketing If You Are an Advertiser.

Affiliate marketing is a promotional strategy that takes place via the Internet and that puts in contact two figures:

- The **Advertiser**, which is the company that wants to promote its products or services. It is also called *merchant*.

- The **Publisher Partner/Affiliate**, which is the person or company who makes his website available for the promotional purposes of the advertiser. Probably you who are reading this book fall into this second category and this is what you aspire to do in the world of affiliate marketing, but for completeness I will also give you a broad overview of the business from the point of view of the advertiser and the advantages also related to this figure, since my goal is to give you, with this guide, a vision as complete as possible of the affiliate marketing business.

Basically, the publisher posts promotional content on their site, and the advertiser pays them a commission for each user who makes a purchase or performs a certain action through that content. That certain action is called in lead marketing jargon and can be for example signing up for a newsletter, watching a video, leaving your phone number to be contacted by a team member and so on.

Affiliate marketing is considered a form of performance-based marketing, because in fact the principal - the advertiser - only pays if he or she gets a certain result, such as a purchase or a lead. As you can easily guess, it is a type of promotion that offers great advantages to both parties involved, but we will talk about that a little later. Instead, let us see now in detail how affiliation works.

How to Start Affiliate Marketing if You Are a Publisher Partner/Affiliate from Scratch

Do you want to become an affiliate marketer? That is a great idea, as this is a huge growth market. Data collected showed that affiliate marketing spend in the UK has increased by 15% annually since 2018 and is steadily rising as the years go by, while in the US it is expected to grow by 62% by 2021. Unfortunately, however, such amazing data is not only known to me and now to you, but it has attracted the attention of thousands of influencers, bloggers, and webmasters, who have jumped into the industry without delay. The affiliate market is worth billions of dollars and new millionaires are popping up like mushrooms everywhere in the world. This means that there is a lot of attention on the subject, but also that you can potentially have a lot of competition, but do not be discouraged, by following the advice I have collected in this book you will be able to gain a good position in the affiliate world and start off on the right foot.

How to do affiliate marketing from scratch?

If you are starting from scratch - that is, if you do not yet have a website, blog, social profile following or newsletter that can attract advertiser interest - the first thing to do is not to listen to your gut. You may think you have come up with a great idea that will bring you tons of views and allow you to make stellar sales for your advertisers. However, at the risk of shattering a dream, I would advise against embarking on any business venture, including affiliation, without having a solid foundation of numbers, data, and information to work from. First you must understand how much competition there is in your potential field, how much traffic social sites/profiles similar to the one you want to create have, what search volume the keywords you want to focus on have. After that, do the products that reference your niche have a growing market? Is it a market that does not just revolve around a passing fad, destined to disappear overnight? Last but not least, is it an area where affiliate programs are plentiful?

To find out how many and what affiliate programs exist in your niche you have three options:

1) Explore the offerings in an established affiliate network.

2) Google "[your niche, for example: "natural beauty products"] + affiliate program. We recommend that no matter where you are in the world, you do your research in English as this will give you access to the global affiliate program market.

3) Search for websites, blogs, and social profiles in your niche, looking for affiliate links in their content and discovering companies and industries that you might be interested in publishing to.

In short, try to gather all the information you can to understand if there is really a place for your idea in the market and if it can bring you the profits you hope for or make you take a wrong step.

If, on the other hand, you already have a well-established social profile, blog, website, or newsletter, it is time to find a way to put value on them, or rather monetize them. Find out what products your audience is interested in and you can find potential advertisers. Think a little outside the box of your niche and try to see things from a broader perspective.

For example: you have an immensely popular YouTube channel where you cover fashion history. At first glance you might think that companies interested in promoting themselves through your channel are mainly from the clothing industry. What you need to ask yourself is: who is your audience? If you mainly attract an audience of young women, then companies interested in starting an affiliate program with you might come from industries such as cosmetics, interior decoration, candles, accessories such as antique jewelry or even video games.

How to Start Affiliate Marketing If You Are an Advertiser

As an advertiser, the world of affiliation opens up a world of promotional possibilities and new ways to reach your audience.

Here are the main ones:

- Bloggers and editorial content: bloggers and editorial sites are one of the best tools for companies that want to start affiliate programs. This is because they know their audience perfectly and can produce great content within which to promote products. Since the products generally tend to be closely related to the content and are targeted to an already quite interested (in jargon "hot") audience, these programs usually bring a great return to companies.

- Coupon sites: 59% of consumers say they are influenced in their purchases more by the presence of coupons than any other form of promotion. It is obvious, all people of any gender nationality or age like to take advantage of discounts. And that's why sites that offer coupons and discount codes are one of the most effective tools for getting new customers.
- Review sites: According to a study by the Spiegel Research Center, reviews greatly influence consumers' purchasing decisions. By now, the vast majority of people who are about to make a purchase, particularly if it involves expensive products, first consult reviews from sources they believe are reliable. That is why sites that publish reviews are among the best affiliate partners.
- Influencers on social media: influencers enjoy the well-established trust of their audience, who see them as reference points, but also in some ways as friends, people with whom they have a personal relationship. This makes them ideal testimonials for your product.
- E-mail marketing: e-mail marketing is a channel of communication that is now less used than it once was, due to the increasingly stringent filters adopted by e-mail providers against spam. For this reason, those who have built a strong credibility over the years thanks to a newsletter are definitely good marketers and can guide your company towards the generation of valuable contacts.

3°. Multiple Benefits for Publishers and Seven Major Benefits for Advertisers

Multiple Benefits for Publishers

Entering an affiliate relationship with one or more companies can be a great way to earn money from your internet business by monetizing your website or social profile. Let us take a few examples. Are you an expert in video games and thanks to this passion you have become a youtuber with a certain following? Well, you could earn money by promoting companies in the industry in your videos, perhaps allowing your audience to take advantage of exclusive discount codes. You will earn a commission; your followers will be able to buy a product at a discounted price and the company will gain new customers. Another example: you are a travel enthusiast and the blog where you talk about your wonderful vacations has a large and loyal audience. Why not finance your next intercontinental flight by simply posting a banner or a link? Or are you an expert sommelier? Why not put your taste for wines to good use by launching a website and getting paid to publish reviews and advice? In short, affiliate marketing is a great way to leverage your success on the web, earning commissions based on the new customers or prospects you bring to companies. Be warned, it is a booming industry in which, as much as USD 12 billion is invested each year.

Seven Major Benefits for Advertisers

Affiliate marketing can bring huge benefits to businesses of any size, but particularly small businesses. There are several reasons for this, and they are all valid.

1. Convenience and Speed

Affiliate marketing is a type of marketing that allows you to obtain great results with a minimal investment. In fact, you pay only if you get the result you want (such as a purchase or a lead), without having to hire a team of professionals but entrusting publishers with the task of disseminating and sometimes even producing your promotional content. This way you can eliminate the risk of an investment in advertising that may not be successful.

The ROI of the affiliate channel is on average 1:18 US dollars. This means that for every dollar you invest, you get $18 back. Plus, the return is typically faster than other marketing strategies. And the volume of traffic generated by affiliation is immense. 16% of all online orders today go through an affiliate link.

2. Reach New Audiences

Publishers will take your message to their audience, and you will reach new niche markets or new areas of the world you haven't explored yet. Want to launch your product in a new country? Reach out to influencers and sites with large audiences that match your goals and start an affiliate program.

3. Track and Measure Results

Affiliate marketing makes it amazingly easy to track and measure the results of your marketing activity, since each link from the publisher to your site contains a specific code. You will be able to know in real time what is working and what is not and adjust your strategy if necessary. With exact numbers in hand, optimizing your advertising spend will be much easier.

4. Improve Reputation and Visibility on the Internet

Affiliate marketing is a great way to improve your internet presence across the board. People will talk about you and your products online, increasing brand awareness of your target audience and boosting your site's SEO. You will be able to stand out from your competitors in a really effective way.

5. Launch New Products with Very Low Risk

You are a young dynamic company that wants to grow and launch new products but cannot afford to risk big advertising investments.

Affiliation is the perfect solution to test your latest creation, approach a new audience or a new market, while limiting the risks as much as possible. In fact, you only pay if you get results. And if the audience responds, you may eventually decide to focus on more "traditional" advertising strategies.

6. Keep Control of Spending

Unlike some forms of pay-per-click advertising, where you can't know in advance how much a lead will cost, with affiliation you are in control of your expenses. You can set a commission for each product, deciding exactly how much you will spend for the result you want to achieve.

7. More Time to Focus on What You Do Best

If you have a business, your job is not to promote your products, but to make them, to improve them, to create new ones. This is what you do best. Affiliation allows you to spend as little time and energy as possible on marketing, which is done by others, for you. Plus, you only pay them if they get results, with no risk.

I want to give you a practical example, recent and concrete to give you an idea of the power of affiliate marketing, a practical case lived in first person. It will certainly help you to better understand one of the many possible ways to earn money. It is a classic example of successful collaboration between publisher and advertiser.

A girl I know, young and with a strong spirit of initiative (in short, a person like you could easily be at the beginning of your entrepreneurial adventure) at his first experience in the world of affiliate marketing has decided to collaborate with a sushi restaurant below home having already a friendly relationship with the owner. The restaurateur was desperate, as with the Covid-19 pandemic he did not know how to keep his business going during the first hard lockdown phase, having almost completely wiped out his income. The situation was profoundly serious indeed as 95% of his income came from customers physically dining at his restaurant. The government of his country had not allocated enough aid to cover his expenses and the contagions continued to rise. His only option was to work with take-away, but he had never organized himself in this regard as it was not his core business. To make matters worse, there was the fact that the restaurateur had no technological experience whatsoever, he was in fact one of those people around 60 years of age who barely surfs the internet. The girl then decided to make available her skills and proposed to the man, through a sponsored-on Facebook, to make a targeted campaign in the city where the restaurant is located, geo localizing it in the area of 100 km from the restaurant, proposing a specific promotion of 30% to be applied when ordering directly on the site, by entering a discount code. They agreed on a percentage for the girl on each sale via coupon, referred to in the link, and started this new collaboration (also because given the dramatic situation, the restaurateur had no other choice or hope). The girl then set to work and in a short time created what in technical jargon is called a catchy "Bonus Page" starting to spread her advertising companion. Do you know how it went? Within three weeks the restaurant went from almost zero turnover to $60,000, with 1,000 orders with an average receipt of $60. The girl, on the other hand, earned $10,000 for her affiliate performance. She told me, in a very funny way, that at one point the owner, almost incredulous, unprepared by the amount of work and struggling to manage so many takeaway orders at once, called her on the phone saying: *"Please, close the site! I cannot handle the orders anymore! Shut it down!"* not having the slightest idea of how the technological world worked. When I think about it, I still smile now. Beyond the funny episode, the purpose of this case study is to give you a concrete example of the potential of the affiliate and how many possible outlets this business can have. If you have a good wit and desire to do, acquired a little experience in the field, you can also propose to store or restaurants or companies in your neighborhood or in your city as a performer with affiliate programs and specific campaigns to improve online sales, or in the case of small reality, to propose a service of web sales to which they are not yet structured or do not have the capacity to do so.

4°. How Can I Make Money with Affiliate Marketing?

The answer to the question "how to make money with affiliate marketing" is the same whether you are a publisher or an advertiser: by building great content and pitching it to the right audience. Here are some questions you should ask yourself to maximize your earnings through an affiliate marketing strategy:

- What is my target audience? Whether you are a business or a blogger, youtuber or other type of publisher, it is imperative to know your audience very well. If you as a business want to target your advertising to the noticeably young, you will need to choose publishers that appeal to this audience. If you are a publisher, you need to find out who your readers or followers are, so you can propose yourself as an affiliate to the right companies.
- How can I leave my readers/followers amazed? It is the so-called "wow effect," the one that makes a potential customer stand in amazement. To achieve this, you need to produce mind-blowing content that will amaze and drive a purchase. Companies can choose whether to create the necessary creativity themselves or create it together with the publisher. Undoubtedly, the latter knows its audience well and how to communicate with them. The beauty of affiliation is that it brings together the creative skills of companies with those of publishers, sometimes generating utterly amazing results.
- If you are a brand, it is crucial to set clear goals for your marketing strategy. Do you want to get sales? Or is what you are interested in is getting a large number of personal contacts from potential customers? And as a publisher, blogger, or influencer, what is the outcome you think you are going to get? Do you think you will be able to drive your followers to purchase, or would you rather get a commission for every click?

Only by sincerely answering all these questions through a meticulous analysis will you be able to choose the most advantageous affiliate program for you.

5°. If I Start from Scratch, How Do I Generate Organic Traffic?

When a person first starts approaching affiliate marketing, one does not know where to start. It is normal. The sense of inadequacy, inability and discouragement can assail you but do not panic. Everyone has started from point zero, including me, and found themselves lost not knowing what to do or in which direction to go. Even the same people who are now making multi-million-dollar royalties every year in affiliate marketing felt the same way you did in the beginning. Always remember, as an old saying goes,"*A long journey always begins with a first step.*"

My job is to help you build a path. To show you the way and above all a business model that can be a profitable winner from an economic point of view.

When we talk about Affiliate marketing we often talk about organic traffic and paid traffic. If paid traffic is easy to understand, I think that organic traffic should be explained a little better, perhaps with examples. Generating organic traffic means creating attention in a natural way on a particular product or service that you are selling, with different channels and tools (websites, articles, posts, or videos on YouTube) to potential customers, so that they can buy your particular good or service. In addition to organic traffic, you can add paid traffic, which is used to increase the visibility of your content to a wider audience, through different platforms (Facebook, Google, Instagram, Tik Tok) through special programs (Google Ads, Facebook Ads).

If you have excellent products or services but no one can see them, it is like having a beautiful painting hidden and packed under your bed that no one can ever admire. Similarly applies if your content or your site. This happens when your site, your blog, stays on page 20 of Google. No one is going to reach it. Just think about a marketplace like Amazon. 90% of worldwide product sales happen on the first page. If your product appears on the third page no one will ever buy it. It is statistically proven. Therefore, it is essential to be visible to as many people as possible and this is done through organic traffic. <u>So, to be successful online and in affiliate marketing, whether you are an advertiser or a publisher, you must adopt a mix of organic traffic in addition to paid traffic.</u>

Maybe at the beginning you have a limited budget, since paid campaigns have costs and they perform better if the higher the investment in the campaign (think, just to give you some numbers that those who earn millions of dollars a year in affiliates also invest $100,000 a month in advertising campaigns), so you must focus your attention initially on generating as much organic traffic as possible. Do not be discouraged if you do not have big budgets, business is built over time. Do not be in a hurry or act on impulse. However, even if you have big capital, I strongly discourage you from investing large sums of money, even if the spread of the campaign would be very extensive to many people. Why? Remarkably simple, you lack the experience. It would be like playing everything on red or black at the Casino. Personally, I do not recommend it. I advise you to adopt a more prudent and gradual business behavior over time. One of the most important aspects when it comes to generating organic traffic is to create credibility, trust with your followers.

Keep in mind that those who follow you, those who read your articles, your blog, those who listen to you on your YouTube channel are not because they like you, or maybe it can be only a small part of the real motivation, that is that the follower simply follows you because he or she needs something. This need may translate into particular and specific information, or technical tools or programs because he wants to create his own business and before buying, he gets informed, reads reviews, listens to opinions. When a customer buys, unless it is an impulse buy, he uses all the channels and networks that technology makes available because he wants to be convinced to make the best and optimal choice. Often those who seek information do so because they want to start a new business, want to solve a problem, or perhaps want to increase their income and often want to do so through the internet. Probably that surfer has come across your article on "*how to make money online*", in your YouTube channel, simply because he wants to buy an article and you have made a video where you are making a review, testing the product, analyzing the positive or negative aspects. The person listening to you expects a review that is simple, understandable, and possibly as unbiased as possible. Potential clients are probably creating their own path, looking for a business model to apply. No one is born with skills in their pocket. You train, you buy training courses, books, or specific programs. It is essential to take care of your training. No one gives anything away in life and especially online.

The goal is to provide useful content, free of charge that can qualitatively improve the lives of your potential customers. Only if potential followers understand that your content is interesting, honest, and improving will they start to follow you. In this way, a path begins where people will see you as competent, trustworthy, and deserving of your trust. They will follow you on your YouTube channels, read your blogs and your posts. Haven't you ever wondered, for example, why when a guru comes out with a new book on a method or a diet or a different strategy everyone runs to buy it? Logical, the authority of that guru is not questioned by those followers. They know they will not be disappointed, and they won't regret their purchase. The same goes for you. Once you have demonstrated that you are prepared, honest, and competent people, then those who read you, those who listen to you in a video will begin to trust you. When someone trusts you, they will automatically be convinced that the product you are talking about is really the right one for them, as they trust you and will follow your advice. So, if you talk about a certain software, listing certain features and the person listening to you and reading you is looking for that particular software, he or she will buy that particular product over other similar ones, because they are convinced of your words.

Now comes the fun part. Where is the gain? Simple, once you have explained the product you will attach in the article or in the YouTube video the affiliate link. In this way, by clicking on your link the customer will go directly to the product page and if you perfect the purchase you will be credited a part of the purchase in the percentage provided by the affiliate program.

Let me give you a practical example.

There are affiliate programs that offer as much as 50% commission on the sale price. If the customer through your link buys a $100 piece of software, $50 will be given to you as a commission. Imagine becoming an authoritative figure in a target industry and having 500,000 subscribers to your channel of people interested in your content. I am not saying it is easy or immediate, I am just determining the potential. Look at the hypothetical of earning $50 by selling a software or good through an affiliate link due to having gained the credibility and trust of thousands of people. Imagine selling a software to 1000 people. $50 royalty (equal to 50% of the price agreed upon by the affiliate program) x 1,000 buyers = $50,000.00. Boom!

Are you starting to understand the huge potential of this business? Are you understanding how people make millions of dollars in royalties every year? Think about promoting 10 products or software every month, the market potential is exorbitant.

Haven't you ever wondered why all these guys in their early twenties open a YouTube channel and keep insisting on subscribing to their channel and liking their videos?

If you analyze them closely, they always talk about products, describe them, and offer you discounts or timed promotional offers in their links below the video. They are doing nothing but affiliate marketing. Maybe, in fact often, they sell a lot of products through affiliate links and make a lot of money in royalties. They have created or are trying to create trust in those who follow or listen to them, they want to become authoritative because they want to turn a simple listener into a "potential customer" and very often they succeed. Welcome to the amazing world of affiliate marketing!

6°. The Seven Steps to Follow to Generate a Commission

Choose a Niche; Build a Site; Search for Affiliate Programs; Create Excellent Content; Build Your Audience; Promote Affiliate Offers; Repeat the Process.

Resuming the concepts already expressed in part, let us see together what the 7 steps are to generate profit with affiliate marketing.

1. Choose a Niche.

Before you even start building your first website, you need to decide what niche you want to target. If you already have that in mind, you are on your way!

This is without a doubt one of the most difficult and vast steps. Of course, there is nothing to stop you from opening up other niches after you've started and started well in one niche. However, it is good to take it one step at a time.

Some key questions to ask yourself when choosing your niche are these:

- What topics am I already passionate about?
- What topics can I easily write 25, 50 or 100 posts on?
- Is there a place in this niche for a new affiliate?
- Is there enough interest/demand for products in this niche?
- Are there affiliate programs available in this niche?

2. Build a Site.

Assuming you have not already built a site, this will be the next step to take. Fortunately, building a website is not as complicated and labor intensive as in the past.

As of today, there are plenty of portals that offer site creation services. Do a minimum of research and evaluate, according to your type of business, the one that you feel is best suited to your needs and budget. However, I allow myself to give you some advice, analyzing some aspects that I think are important, before making a final choice and these are:

- Free Trial. Make sure you can try the free site creator first. Many providers offer free packages (with some limitations) or at least a money back option.
- Support. Check what kind of support is offered (if its phone makes sure it's 7 days a week, email support, chat, forums, etc.). It is also worth knowing if there is a community of users who can help each other.
- Price. It is a bit tricky to define because sometimes offers can be confusing. But in all our reviews you will find clear details of each package and extra costs (e.g., for the domain) for each site creator.
- Features. Obviously, each project will have different needs. But there are some common elements that probably interest you too: a blog, customizable in-click SEO options, responsive design, a shopping cart, good image galleries, the ability to have password-protected pages or have registered users.
- Domain. You should be able to connect a domain purchased elsewhere, although you have the option to register one directly with the site creator.

3. Search for Affiliate Programs.

Now that you have chosen a niche, and your site is up and running, it is time to find products to promote.

Choosing an affiliate program will take some work, but do not be afraid to invest some time in it. It will be worth it to choose the right program!

When choosing an affiliate program, keep these aspects in mind:

- Products should have more than 50% commission (preferably 60%) and have a high ranking (this means they are in demand).
- For CPA (cost per action) programs, commissions are around $1 and not overly restrictive on how you can promote them.
- For physical products, look for commissions over $40.

Once you have decided which programs to use, sign up and move on to step number 4.

4. Create Excellent Content.

Now that your site is up and running and you are part of an affiliate program, you are finally ready to start the most time-consuming (but potentially the most rewarding) part of producing affiliate content.

This is where the overused but truer-than-ever phrase comes into play: "*Content is king.*" Your goal will be to turn the site into an authority in your niche, and the most effective way to do that is to create fresh, unique, high-quality content.

This is likely to consist of:

- Product reviews.
- Posts that talk about common problems, questions, or relevant issues in the marketplace.
- Timeless content.
- Free e-books and videos.
- A professional autoresponder for email marketing.

5. Build Your Audience.

Acquiring an audience for your site is a step that will happen naturally once you have produced excellent content. There are a few ways to do this faster, including:

- Promote your content on Social Media (Facebook, Twitter, Google+, etc.).
- Write guest posts on popular blogs.
- Building an email list (where you can promote your content).
- Use simple SEO techniques to increase traffic to your site through search engines.

You can also consider requesting not-too-expensive banner ads on small niche sites or try your hand at Google AdWords to drive some traffic to your site.

6. Promote Affiliate Offers.

Once you have proven that you offer quality content in your niche, it is time to continue adding quality by promoting products that will be useful and helpful to your audience.

You can do this by providing detailed product reviews, promoting on banner ads or with pop-ups on your site, working with affiliate programs by offering giveaways or contests, or giving discounts to your readers on affiliate products.

It is only a matter of time before you can complete your first sale.

7. Repeat the Process.

Your job as an affiliate marketer involves repeating steps 4 through 6 continuously and tirelessly.

It may seem like an immense amount of work to do everything you need to do to bring your site to life and build your reputation. But once you have made your first sale, and I guarantee that getting your first sale is a thrill as well as a great satisfaction, you will want to sell every day forever. As you have just seen, there is a real and proven strategy for Affiliate Marketing beginners. Put in the work and you will soon reap success.

7°. On Which Products Can You Earn More with Affiliate Marketing?

What products should you focus on for affiliate marketing?

Certainly, software has much higher percentages than physical products/materials that can reach from 50 to 80% of the total value. Why a software returns so much compared to physical products? The answer is intuitable: a software once created has no more costs. If I promote a physical product, instead, the company will have a cost linked to the production and purchase of every single product that each time I go to promote. A remarkably interesting sector are also the subscriptions related to software, because once expired, generally after a year from the purchase, if the user is satisfied, he will renew the subscription, and this will generate an automatic income. However, I want to point out that not all beginners should go and promote technological products. especially in cases in which you do not have any competence in the field, or you do not even have any specific interest in the subject. If you are a wine expert, does it make sense to promote software just because they give high commissions? Absolutely not. For what reason? You are not authoritative, and this is perceivable, and, above all, it will be understood by whoever listens to you. Whoever hears you will not perceive enthusiasm, emotional involvement. If you explain a product as if you were reading television programming to your grandmother, you will hardly succeed in making your mark and converting a listener into a potential client. If you do not like the topic, it will become much more difficult and most likely you will not get results. You will only run the risk of wasting time and not making money. If you do not believe yourself in the product you are promoting, how can you convince others?

In case you are a wine expert you will be able to transmit all your enthusiasm, your passion by promoting wines, by using your experience in order to value the qualities, the organoleptic properties of the product, taste, color and everything else you can do with, such as the matching with food. You will surely earn much more money by proposing affiliate links on wine bottles, rather than on software links to increase organic traffic.

This example is meant to make you realize that you need to focus on the area you are most confident about. You do not have to be in software at all costs. That would be like doing a job you do not like. You would have the same catastrophic results, lose enthusiasm, and eventually quit. Focus, especially in the beginning, on what you are passionate about. Do not try to imitate others, follow your own path. For example, if you are a normal guy, used to dress casually in jeans and t-shirts, do not make videos renting luxury cars or sprinkling yourself with bills and huge golden necklaces as if you were a rapper promoting his music video, because this image does not belong to you. That would be ridiculous and counterproductive. Above all, the audience will understand it.

Or are you girls and have a passion for make up? Great, then pursue this avenue, make deals with perfumeries and cosmetic stores in the area. Make blogs on tips for how to do the best makeup. Make videos, posts, articles where you analyze the products, explain what type of skin is best for a certain cream or recommend a new color of lipstick for the next season. People will start to follow you and buy the products you are sponsoring. Create empathy. This example is meant to make you realize that you need to focus on the area you are most confident about. You do not have to be in software at all costs. That would be like doing a job you do not like. You would have the same catastrophic results, lose enthusiasm, and eventually quit. Focus, especially in the beginning, on what you are passionate about. Do not try to imitate others, follow your own path. For example, if you are a normal guy, used to dress casually in jeans and t-shirts, do not make videos renting luxury cars or sprinkling yourself with bills and huge golden necklaces as if you were a rapper promoting his music video, because this image does not belong to you. That would be ridiculous and counterproductive. Above all, the audience will understand it. Or are you girls and have a passion for make up? Great, then pursue this avenue, make deals with perfumeries and cosmetic stores in the area. Make blogs on tips for how to do the best makeup. Make videos, posts, articles where you analyze and try on yourself the products, explain what type of skin is best for a certain moisturizer or recommend a new color of lipstick for the next season. People will start to follow you and buy the products you are sponsoring. Create empathy. Of course, in the beginning you can take inspiration or even copy certain methods already used by industry gurus such as famous make-up artists, then you will create your own style.

If you decide to expose yourself at the forefront and think you will be more effective by opening a YouTube channel, you should not be afraid to show your weaknesses. Do not get stuck if your videos are not perfect the first few times. Do not go into a performance panic, you get better with time. Remember that people do not follow you, but the content you offer them. They do not care if you are tall, short, thin, fat, beautiful, ugly, young, or old. Well, of course it is helpful to look your best, by that I mean that it is enough to show up with clean hair, a fresh and rested face, an outfit that does not grab too much attention and other basic tricks. You do not have to have any kind of "inferiority complex" if there is someone else who is cooler or trendier than you. Everyone creates their own path. In the world of the web there is room for everyone, and you are not in competition with anyone, only with yourself with your ambitions and your goals. Remember that a user reads one of your articles, puts the "like" or the "I follow you" to your channel because he/she believes that you can be useful for his/her path. You are a means to the results that those who listen to you want to obtain. Then of course, with time you can become a reference figure, an authoritative person, a person worthy of esteem and trust or "family" by those who follow you.

If your followers trust you, they will look forward to reading your new article, seeing your new post, or watching your new YouTube video.

Then, sure, you definitely need to be empathetic as well, and express yourself clearly and honestly. If you have a strong local accent, try to "smooth" it out as much as possible. You do not need to take a diction class, just speak with a clean voice. No one wants to see a video of a boring person with a monotone voice, a microphone that croaks or mishears and a video with horrible graphics. Imagine starting a video made by a zombie-faced guy who talks like he has a potato in his mouth unless you are a masochist you will quickly move on. The same if you run into a generic article, not very attractive from the graphic point of view or with banal contents and maybe even with embarrassing grammatical errors. Quality, as already stated in the previous chapters, is an especially important aspect.

Let me add a further step that I think is important.

Besides trust, people buy products or services through you not because they like you, but because they have a competitive advantage. For example, "If you sign up for this Blockchain platform via my link and buy $100 worth of cryptocurrency, you'll get $30 off." This is the winning lever. The platform wins because it has a new customer who has invested $100 in the platform and will buy and sell cryptocurrencies from there on out (and the platform will earn a commission on all future trades the customer makes). You won because you took a royalty percentage from the affiliate link and the customer won because they signed up for a blockchain platform, which they wanted to do, but saved $30.

Why should the customer buy from you if they have no real benefit? So here he is serving up promotions, discounts, promos, coupons, price cuts, seasonal offers and so on. Boom!!! Win to Win.

8°. The Best Portals for Affiliate Programs

ClickBank; Warrior Plus; JVZOO; Builderall; Siteground, Hostgator and Godaddy; Fiverr; Amazon.

Now let us see where you can actually start applying for affiliate links. Again, I premise that these are my indications that serve only to give you a list of portals aimed to help you in your search, that I use and that I know personally. It is up to you, however, then analyze them and get into the merits, do research, and identify the most suitable according to your path, your industry, and the type of business you are going to do in the affiliate marketing.

This is not an exhaustive list, but an indicative one and feel free to use any other affiliate site, also because there are many, including some specific to the state or continent in which you are, and it is therefore difficult to list them all.

ClickBank

ClickBank is a highly respected Affiliate Network, among the most prominent in the industry. It has been in existence since 1998, has over 200 million customers worldwide and claims to have created over 1000 millionaire members through its platform. Here you will find many niches and topics where you can promote and affiliate. Just to give you some additional information, the online education industry (most digital products fall into this category) is in full swing and worth well over $100 billion worldwide. As anticipated, the affiliate marketing industry is on the rise. In the United States alone, spending on this industry will exceed $8 billion by 2022. Some of the advantages of this affiliate network definitely include:

- A reliable affiliate network.

- A wide range of products in every niche.

- An attractive commission structure for affiliates.

- Easy to get started.

- Weekly or bi-weekly payment methods.

- Detailed background information and comprehensive training on usage thanks to Clickbank University.

<u>Warrior Plus</u>

Warrior plus is among the most popular affiliate networks in the world, and it is extremely easy to sign up. If you want, you just need a common PayPal account to receive affiliate payments and the links are really interesting. This is a platform, unlike ClickBank, more specific for software or product info. Also, here the commissions are interesting. Unlike ClickBank here you need to apply for permission to be accepted by sellers and the affiliate link is not granted automatically. Especially if you are new and just starting out, your applications may not be accepted or remain pending for quite some time. They do this because those who launch their products are usually not very keen on giving their affiliate link to those they don't consider experienced or new to the industry.

So, how do you overcome this problem that you often run into in the beginning?

My advice is to contact the seller via Facebook (you can usually find the name, contact and a picture in the product tab).

I suggest you take your phone and make a short but good video presentation of a few minutes such as:

"Hi (SELLER'S NAME) I'm (YOUR NAME) here. I am trying to promote your (PRODUCT NAME) on (DATE).

I will be sending my traffic from my YouTube channel.

I know the correct way to promote products.

I would like you to kindly approve my affiliate link. I will be grateful.

See you soon. Bye."

If you do not want to make a video (or think it is not appropriate for other reasons) you can easily write to the seller, even if the video of a few minutes is absolutely the most effective way to get the affiliate link.

Here you will find for each product that will be launched the relative Funnel with the description, usually incredibly detailed of the product features, the launch date, and the various offers, with a price that usually includes a basic package and the various up grades, with different price ranges. Usually, those who sell this type of products through affiliate links, being software and technical products are usually making video reviews on YouTube of the product to better explain its functionality. Why is this done? That' s simple.

Whoever wants to buy a certain software is used to read and compare as many reviews as possible to be sure that the product works well and above all wants to try to understand more about its potential. Therefore, before buying a product that "increases traffic" the average customer will simply go to YouTube, put "product name+review" in the search engine. Here the user will see your video and if you are credible and explain the functionality of the software in a serious and professional way the customer will buy the product directly from your affiliate link, which you will put below your video. Usually, the most experienced salespeople are used to buying the software and using it during the video, sharing the screen during the explanation. This creates more credibility in those who see you and will greatly increase the likelihood of a purchase as seeing yourself explaining the software and using it greatly increases the credibility on the real potential of the product. Similarly, seeing a girl explain a certain type of makeup while applying it on her face showing step by step the result and texture or smell of a skin foundation, will have much more impact than a video of a girl showing herself without makeup.

JVZOO

A remarkably similar platform to Warrior Plus, is definitely JVZOO.

Here too for the affiliate link you will have to be authorized by the seller. The same rules and the same procedure of WarriorPlus apply.

If in addition to promoting products of others you want to make and sell their products, platforms such as JVzoo and Warrior Plus for the registration does not provide for the payment of a monthly or annual fee, with the ability to sell your products at no cost (the percentage deducted from sales in favor of the portal is still marginal). This is an advantage over platforms like ClickBank that ask for a fee (about $50, but it is subject to change), to set up your product in the platform, regardless of how the online sale will go. The benefit is that the greatest American marketers are selling their experience and expertise to anyone who wants to follow them. In JvZoo, as well as in ClickBank, every single user has the possibility to create his own digital product and put it on sale, establishing a percentage of earnings to all those who are interested in reselling their creation.

Builderall

Builderall is a new and constantly evolving platform that provides all the tools every marketer needs to sell online. Some examples are creation of Landing Page, Funnel, Email Marketing, Graphics, Facebook Bot and much more... The affiliate program provided by this platform is one of the most profitable. In fact, it provides 100% commission on the first purchase + 30% at each renewal (so recurring commissions). In addition, if the people who have purchased from you, have affiliates (Tier 2) you will earn an additional 30% of their earnings (each month).

Siteground, Hostgator and Godaddy

If you work on the web, promoting web hosting services could be interesting.

Almost all web hosting services offer an affiliate program, the percentages are usually around 40%, others pay a fixed fee for each membership that usually starts from 40/50dollars to go up. Not bad I would say.

Fiverr

Fiverr is one of the largest and most famous portals in the world where you can find freelancers for any kind of job. Fiverr's affiliate program is nothing short of extraordinary, as well as highly profitable. There are different ways to earn money, the most common one is definitely the CPA one, where you just need the user to sign up and purchase any product. Here the commissions range from 15USD to 150USD per single lead. The affiliate panel is one of the most complete and accurate I have ever seen, full of creativity, widgets and much more. This will make it easier and more profitable. Another thing that makes the Fiverr affiliate program extremely beneficial is its versatility, in fact, the niches are so numerous that you can promote this platform whatever your industry is. To sign up, all you have to do is click on the link above and fill out the form. In most cases you will be immediately accepted, and you will be able to start selling right away.

Amazon

Joining Amazon is easy and free, for sure the earning percentages are not remarkably high, in fact they reach a maximum of about 10%, but selling products on this portal is extremely easy as Amazon is an authoritative brand that people trust. This marketplace really sells everything, so it is great for any niche.

An unpleasant aspect of Amazon is the absence of cookie tracking, in fact the user is forced to buy something (not necessarily the product promoted by you) within the active session, if he decides to conclude the purchase the next day by making a new login, the commission will not be credited.

9°. Why is a Funnel More Important than a Website?

A website is generally used to show the world that we are online, we are present in the digital landscape.

It usually consists of several pages (blog pages excluded) where all the important information about our business is included, for example:

- About Us
- Our Services
- Products Showcase
- Our Blog

Visitors therefore have a variety of choices. There is no precise focus, each page leads to other different pages and there is no single path to follow.

A website is definitely a great way to generate traffic especially organic if we have worked well with SEO. Just to specify, in case you were not aware, SEO is a branch of Web Marketing that deals with the optimization of a website for search engines. The term SEO is in fact an acronym for Search Engine Optimization, literally optimization for search engines.

The goal of SEO activity is to climb the positions on the search engine results pages (the SERPs) for certain keywords, in order to intercept and attract users interested in a particular product, service or information, providing them with relevant content.

<u>However, the website has a noticeably big problem and that is what we will focus on: an incredibly low conversion rate.</u>

A more effective method of increasing conversion rates provides us with the creation of a Funnel.

At this point the question arises: **<u>what are funnels and why are they so important?</u>**

Funnels are one of the most potential business and marketing opportunities.

A funnel is a sales process that guides a potential customer through a series of pages. This way you can tell why they should buy your product and you can prepare ad-hoc offers such as upsells and cross-sells. Everything remains obviously aimed at the three main goals of a website: <u>find new leads, sell more, and increase profits.</u>

Funnels are a powerful marketing tool that can therefore be used to:

- Funnels are a powerful marketing tool that can be used therefore to:
- Sell your product.
- Increase newsletter subscribers.
- Create a membership or reserved area for customers.
- Organize a webinar or online course.

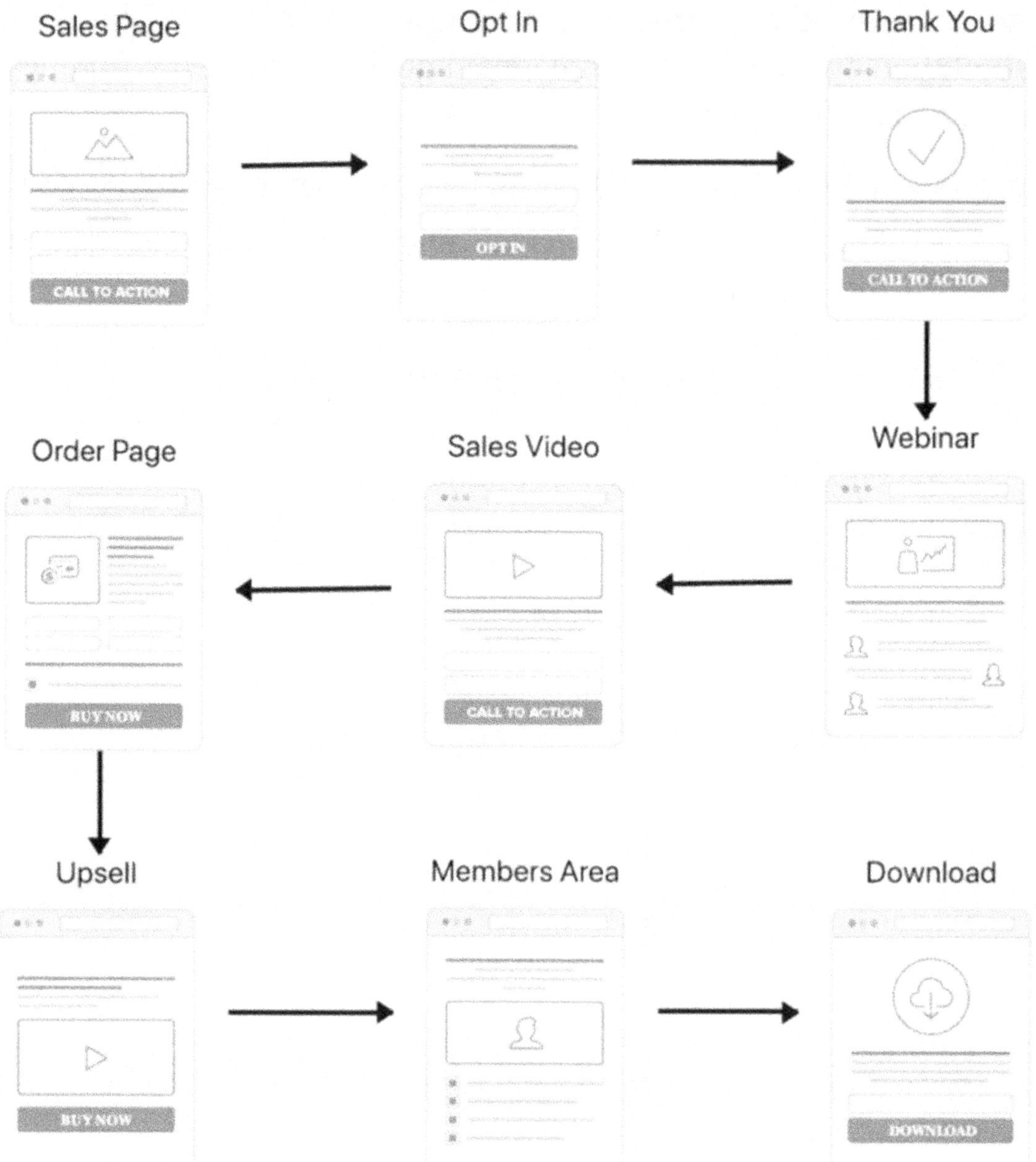

Continuing with the example of the road ahead for our visitor, in the case of the funnel we have road signs. We can guide the visitor to a specific destination. Each page of our Funnel guides the visitor to a precise page that is the next one and that is approaching one step at a time towards achieving our goal. The funnel in short, is a system that allows us to acquire and convert a single customer multiple time.

Do you know what the most problematic aspect of operating online is?

The declining attention span of potential customers. Have you ever wondered why you have hundreds or thousands of visitors, but your sales still struggle to take off? It does not matter how much you have spent to build your Website or your E-commerce: you only have 7 seconds to capture your visitor's attention and convince them to buy from you. It is statistically proven.

According to a well-established statistic to capture the attention of a visitor your positioning must be perceived within the first 10 seconds of navigation. So, a visitor will quickly leave a website if there is nothing to attract their attention. And you will not get a second chance to make a good impression. A website can have the most beautiful design in the world, but it will always be at risk of being lost.... So, if you are selling a product or service online now, you should make sure that you stretch a visitor's attention span as much as possible so that you can generate new leads, sell more, and increase your profits. Creating compelling funnels is the best way to achieve your goals.

10°. Which Are the Main Platforms For Creating Funnels?

ClickFunnels; GetResponse; HubSpot; Kajabi; Leadpages; WishPond.

My goal in this paragraph is to list to you, in a completely unbiased way, a series of platforms, among the most popular and that are for me more familiar and known that deals with the creation of Funnels. It will then be up to you to analyze one by one, step by step, to understand which one is the most suitable to your needs, the one that seems the easiest or intuitive to use or the one that has a pricing plan, more suitable to your spending capacity. Usually, all these platforms have a monthly cost. It will be up to you to choose the option you think is best. My task here is just to give you an overview to facilitate your search, to have a starting point, with a minimum of basic information. Surely there will be many other platforms that are just as good. Do not consider them as an exhaustive list and feel free to do all the research you need on the best Funnel creation program. Enjoy!

ClickFunnels

Among the main platforms for the creation of funnels there is certainly ClickFunnels, which in a couple of years has collected significant numbers. 93,244 users, 913 Million Leads, 5.5 Million Funnels created, 3.8 Billion sales generated.

This platform is quite as easy to use as any similar resource available. The platform has tools to guide buyers through every step of the sales process, such as email and marketing automation through Facebook, and an accessible and fluid web page editor.

GetResponse

GetResponse is an excellent resource for businesses looking for a service that can automate and perform most sales channeling functions on its own. The software boasts impressive features, including Facebook and Instagram ad buying resources, integrated webinar software, and templates for conversion-focused sales pages.

HubSpot

HubSpot platform features include conventional sales channeling tools such as landing page templates, infrastructure for creating and distributing content offers, and email automation.

On top of that, HubSpot's growth platform has everything you need to meet all of your company's marketing, sales and service needs. It is an excellent resource for attracting, engaging, delighting, and retaining customers.

Kajabi

Among the most popular platforms is definitely Kajabi.

Kajabi's solutions are great for increasing interest in your product or service and turning that interest into sales and new customers. Kajabi's platform may not be suitable for small business and startup budgets, as the monthly subscription cost is quite high, but it is still an incredibly effective option for facilitating your sales channeling strategy.

Leadpages

Leadpages is one of the most affordable sales funnel creation solutions available. It can be a good investment for small and medium-sized businesses, young startups and entrepreneurs looking to expand their web presence and acquire new business. If you are looking for an affordable funneling software, Leadpages is a good place to start.

WishPond

WishPond has options that fit the needs and budgets of businesses that are just starting out, but in no way is the software specific to small businesses. It is an impressive platform that boasts an equally impressive list of clients, including Sony, CBS, and Walmart. It is a good option for businesses of any size looking for a comprehensive tool.

11°. Landing Page - Opt-In Page - Squeeze Page - Thank You Page - Sales Pages. What are they?

Everyone telling you in YouTube videos or industry articles, "*Make a super cool landing page!*" or "*It's critical to have a Squeeze page to be successful.*" or "*Opt-in page is everything*". I remember well when, with a strong desire to understand more about how to do affiliate marketing, I was studying books, videos and articles and came across these recurring phrases. I am not ashamed to say that I used to get discouragement and a great sense of loss. It happened to me several times, especially in the beginning and I imagine it happens to you too, despite the curiosity and desire to find out more about this business. But do not panic. Weaknesses and moments of despondency happen to everyone. It is part of custom and human nature. The point is that it is not you who are unsuitable, but rather it is that often those who produce information material take it for granted that those on the other side already know everything, as if instead of people who want to learn from the beginning you are already gurus or super marketing experts. They all provide information in cascades, but no one ever explains to you in an understandable way and starting from the basics what certain functions are and what they are for. Probably, who is in the industry is reluctant to give you too much information and keeps it partly for himself or shares it only in a webinar or in a paid masterclass. In some respects, you cannot blame this behavior. Other times there are also technical needs to make videos or articles of short duration (and consequently the info is given in a superficial way) because if not people are bored, and brevity is also a way to capture attention. I think this is normal. How many times have you put a book back on the shelf because it had 600 pages? Unless you are an avid reader, the idea of having to read so many pages often put you off starting that book. How many times do you not watch a video on Instagram because it is longer than 5 or 10 minutes? With all that said, let us do some deeper analysis.

Landing Page

The landing page is a web page specifically created to convert visitors into leads, which are then potential customers. It is based on the principle of offering the user something attractive that convinces him to leave his data (name, email, etc.) through a simple form. Once the data is provided, it will be time to send him your offers or other interesting content. The landing page then basically serves to convert simple users into end customers.

<u>How does an effective landing page works?</u>

Here is a brief example: we are a pharmacy, and the user accesses a post about influence written on our blog. Once read the post, the user wants to have more information, so he clicks on a call-to-action of an e-book titled "How to Prevent Flu in the Cold Season" that will direct him to our landing page. On the landing page the user is then asked to enter the name and email in order to download the content, and, subsequently, will be redirected to a thank you page, the famous "thank you page" with the download link, thus becoming a valuable lead.

The final result of the landing page will be a list of people really interested in the content of the e-book. This valuable list can then be reused for a targeted advertising campaign.

What is the Squeeze Page? Are there any differences with the Opt-in Page?

The squeeze page is a special landing page.

Squeeze page comes naturally from the English verb "to squeeze", that is to squeeze. Well yes, squeeze the user until the last drop, figuratively speaking of course. Squeeze it until it becomes a Customer with a capital "C".

<u>Between squeeze page and opt-in page there are no differences.</u>

The two are synonymous and indicate a page where the user gives his email address in exchange for a fantastic gift (called "freebee" or "lead magnet").

The gift must be really useful: a pdf, a video, a podcast, a coupon, a freebie or anything else that can give value to your Brand.

<u>How does an effective squeeze page work?</u>

Here is a brief example: we are a shoe store, and our site is little known.

For one day, we propose to our customers to download and print a 30% discount coupon to use in the store directly from the squeeze page of the site.

We thus get 3 benefits:

- The customer definitely returns to the store.
- It creates a relationship of loyalty with the customer.
- We got a new email address to put on the list that we will use for future sponsorships.

<u>How many types of squeeze pages exist?</u>

There are several types of squeeze pages:

- URL Address: a page similar to a landing page or website page.
- Pop Up: the bar that appears while you are browsing a website. Although very annoying, pop ups get a high number of signups.
- Exit Intent: squeeze pages that appear when a user is about to exit the site.

A squeeze page can also be included in a widget placed in the side or end bar of our site. If instead your interest is to sell everything and immediately, you just must rely on a sales page.

<u>Sales Page</u>

A sales page is a page created for the sole purpose of selling a product/service. While the squeeze page must be short, the sales page allows you to provide more information to ensure maximum transparency of the product/service to the user.

Effective squeeze pages and sales pages. Let us see what is good to avoid.

To make a really effective squeeze page (also known as an opt-in page) or sales page, don't make these 3 mistakes:

- **<u>Avoid External Links</u>**. It is essential to avoid links from other sites on your squeeze or sales page, because they risk distracting the reader and making him leave earlier than expected without having left his email address.
- **<u>Ask for As Little Data as Possible</u>**. In reference to the squeeze page, the golden rule is the more fill-in fields you ask for, the lower the sign-up rate. So, weigh carefully what information you are really interested in and leave the rest alone.
- **<u>Do not Underestimate the Power of The Word</u>**. Texts have an extraordinarily strong influence on people only if they are written in the right way. An effective copywriting can attract the user to leave their email address more than many other "incredible" tools.

12°. The Power of Email Marketing and How It Can Help You Get Your Business Off the Ground

One of the most important aspects to grow and make the leap into the affiliate marketing industry, and consequently significantly increase your earnings, is email marketing. Owning a large number of emails and building a solid email list over time will represent a very important asset, your real treasure and the real added value for those who engage in this business. In 1978, Gary Thuerk of Digital Equipment Corporation sent the first mass email to about 400 customers. Thuerk claimed to have generated $13 Million in sales from that email, revealing the high potential of email marketing.

Today, email marketing remains one of the most effective ways to promote brands and engage with leads and customers. Since Thuerk's first email, email marketing campaigns have evolved from being simple mass emails to strategic and highly targeted messages. In this chapter, we will dive into the world of email marketing and discover how your brand can use this tool to increase engagement and growth.

Email marketing is an effective digital marketing strategy that involves sending emails to current and potential customers. This valuable tactic can be used for a variety of purposes, including driving conversions, promoting products, or generating interest in your brand.

While it is obviously not big news, it must be acknowledged that email is and still remains a key strategic channel for almost every industry. For all intents and purposes, it is one of the most effective ways to convert users into customers. In fact, research shows that businesses receive an average ROI (Return of Investment) of $42 for every dollar spent on email marketing. Think, data in hand, the importance of this tool, which is crucial for both advertisers and publishers.

Benefits of Email Marketing

Marketing emails can fulfill different purposes for your business or organization, depending on their content. The main benefits include:

- Promoting products or services.

- Create engagement with the brand.
- Driving traffic to the website.
- Turn leads into customers.
- Turning one-time buyers into repeat customers.

Email definitely has advantages over other forms of communication. First, users are more likely to read an email than a social media post. Second, email allows you to send different messages based on the individual wants and needs of your mailing list subscribers. Compared to universal marketing campaigns, this form of targeted communication is much more effective at generating conversions.

Types of Marketing Emails

From automated emails to weekly newsletters, different types of messages achieve different goals for your brand. You can use a combination of multiple goals to create a comprehensive email marketing strategy.

- Advertising emails are sent with a specific purpose, whether to promote a special offer, encourage users to download a digital product or eBooks, or sign up for a free trial.

- Newsletters are sent on an ongoing basis to provide regular updates to subscribers. A newsletter might share new blog posts or case studies, discuss a product update or milestone just reached, or feature upcoming events.

- Automated email marketing consists of emails that are sent automatically based on predefined triggers. For example, you could send a welcome email to new subscribers, an email to subscribers celebrating their birthdays, and a reminder email to customers with abandoned carts. Or you could send a drip campaign (I explain this more in the next chapter) that can cultivate leads and convince them to buy.

- Automated transactional emails are another effective form of marketing automation and are sent automatically after a transaction. They include order confirmations, shipping updates, and reminders about appointments or events. Although these emails are fairly simple, they are important for building customer trust, especially for ecommerce sites.

13°. What Is Drip Marketing and Why Is It So Important?

If you want to make a splash in your industry, you need a marketing strategy that nurtures your audience over time. That is where marketing automation, specifically drip marketing, comes in. With a name that calls to mind the tranquility of falling raindrops (drip=drop), a drip-type marketing automation campaign includes a series of emails scheduled over the course of several days. This strategy tends to generate more engagement, and consequently drive more conversions, than traditional email marketing.

<u>So, what is a drip campaign?</u>

A drip campaign is a form of marketing automation that is most commonly used for email marketing. With this method, a series of pre-written, pre-programmed emails are sent to your contacts over an extended period of time. The timing of each automation email is based on pre-defined triggers. For example, you can schedule a particular email to be sent to users after they subscribe and a second email 3 days later. This way, you will send your message in gradual "drops", adapting your communication strategy to your audience's behavior.

There are several advantages to sending drip campaigns via automation. First, they help you build engagement from your contacts over time, without being too intrusive and creating interest incrementally rather than overwhelming them with an aggressive campaign. Because drip emails are targeted and personalized, they tend to be more compelling to users than a single email. Ultimately, this technique can lead to fewer unsubscribes and an increased conversion rate.

Second, drip emails increase engagement by keeping your business ever-present in the minds of your audience. They represent a kind of ongoing conversation about your brand, establishing trust over time and gently guiding users through the sales funnel.

<u>Which marketing automation platform is best to use?</u>

The most convenient way to create marketing automation with email is to do it directly through your professional website. This way, you will be able to keep all the information about your business, from site data to email marketing campaigns, organized on one platform.

<u>What are the different types of email automation campaigns?</u>

Email automation sequences are useful in a variety of scenarios, whether you're following up with a customer after a subscription or getting them to buy items from your online store.

Here are some examples of the types of marketing automation campaigns you can create:

- <u>Welcome emails</u>: create automated welcome emails when a user signs up, subscribes, or requests a free trial of your products or services. Let them know you are happy to have them on your site and introduce them to your company's products and services to create an excellent first impression of your brand.
- <u>Organize lead nurturing campaigns</u>: write a series of lead nurturing emails that, over time, convince potential customers to buy. This can include educating users about your industry or offering free trials and consultations. As you move users toward the final part of the sales funnel, consider different ways to engage them with your product, such as getting them to sign up for a webinar or download your app.
- <u>User engagement campaigns</u>: messages that invite users back to your site. For example, you might want to send an email that says, "*We miss you*" to subscribers who have not interacted with your brand in a while, or an email like "You might also be interested in..." that entices them to browse other offers.
- <u>Email for abandoned carts</u>: create email automation campaigns that re-engage customers, especially those with full carts that have not yet checked out. Cart abandonment is a huge problem - in fact, the average percentage of users who abandon their carts before making a purchase approaches 80% - and email automation can reactivate the buying process. To close sales, target customers with a series of powerful automated advertising messages that bring them back to view the

abandoned cart.

- <u>Renewal emails</u>: send customers a renewal reminder if your product runs on a subscription basis. If renewal is automatic, send a notification to users informing them that their account will be charged with an automated pre-filled email. If not, alert them that their subscription is about to expire and create a marketing automation campaign that invites users to re-subscribe to your service.
- <u>Confirmation email</u>: create a confirmation email that not only thanks customers for their purchases, but also generates ongoing engagement. After sending the thank you email, for example, consider creating engagement with marketing automation that promotes new product features or extra accessories.
- <u>Step-by-step tutorials</u>: create a series of mini trainings to share your expertise and generate traffic to your site. By offering subscribers a full set of marketing automation, rather than a sequence of unrelated emails, you can generate interest and engagement with your brand. Try repurposing blog content as a multi-part course sent via email, whether it is a quick SEO tutorial or a series of social media marketing tips.

14°. How to Set Up A Marketing Automation Campaign

Are you ready to create a drip campaign?

Great. Here are the top tips on how to get started:

1.Identify Your Main Objective

2.Determine Your Target Audience

3.Plan Your Campaign

4.Create Compelling Content

5.Start the Campaign

1. Identify Your Main Goal

Whether you are eager to get new leads or want to create word of mouth about your brand, it is important to have a clear goal in mind when creating your marketing automation campaigns. To define your goal, think about what actions you would like your audience to take by the end of the drip campaign. Do you want them to buy a product? Have them sign up for a free trial? Have them interact with your site?

If identifying a specific goal is difficult, here are some ideas to inspire you:

- Promote a product.
- Make sales.
- Create awareness around the brand.
- Increase interaction with your brand.
- Increase the number of subscriptions and registrations.

Once you have chosen your goal, jot it down somewhere. This will serve as your roadmap for the entire marketing automation campaign.

2. Determine Your Target Audience

Marketing automation is not a magic formula that works for everyone;

instead, you will find yourself achieving your goals more consistently if your messages appear personal and relevant in the eyes of your audience. With this in mind, be sure to create different emails for specific subsets of your target market.

This process, called market segmentation, involves dividing your audience into different types of customers based on the characteristics they have in common. These characteristics can be anything from demographics to site behavior to purchase history. Based on this information, you will want to create triggers that determine which campaigns you will send to which users.

For example, you could create a trigger for abandoned carts. In this case, your segment might be people who have not returned to view their cart for a period of at least 24 hours. You should then create an email automation campaign specifically for this segment, with the goal of closing the sale. Another goal might be to increase the number of users who subscribe to your newsletter again. In this case, you should create a segment that represents new subscribers. You should then send a great welcome email to users who fall into that category.

3. Plan the Campaign

Once you have decided what your goal is for sending automated emails and which users to target, you will need to think about how many emails to create and especially how often to send them. On one hand, you want to keep your audience interested and create constant engagement. On the other, you do not want to annoy them by sending too much content. Effective email automation campaigns range from 4 to 10 emails, with anywhere from 3 days to 2 weeks between messages. You may want to leave a time period of only 3-4 days between the first few emails, so you can engage users right out of the gate. After that, allow a little more time between the emails you send to avoid overloading your contacts. Keep in mind that while there are some practices to follow, there are no magic numbers that work for everyone. After you send out your first few marketing automation campaigns, analyze the data and adjust the amount and timing of your emails until you reach the right compromise. Always keep an eye on the calendar of course, check the seasons and if there are crucial appointments such as for example Christmas or other important public holiday in between sending emails and distinguish holidays or weekdays.

4. Create Compelling Content

Once you have defined your goals, determined your segments and triggers, and planned the timing of your marketing automation, you will need to think about content. When writing emails, aim to write content that is useful, interesting, and will drive readers to the desired action. Here are some tips for creating effective content:

- <u>Write effective email subject lines</u>: the first step to a successful marketing automation campaign is getting people to open the message.
- <u>Be personal</u>: people are more interested and engaged when they feel your emails are directed at them. Use audience segmentation to determine which messages and promotions are likely to catch the attention of which groups. Then, customize your marketing automation accordingly.
- <u>Use a tone that is consistent with the brand</u>: brands, like people, have personalities. Help your contacts get to know - even love - your brand by building a memorable brand identity. You can do this by adopting a particular tone of voice in your emails, whether it is a fun, professional and authoritative tone or somewhere in between. Clearly, it depends on what the nature of your business is.
- <u>Be concise</u>: do not overwhelm your subscribers with too much information or large blocks of text. Make sure to keep your message short and with plenty of space to make it easily digestible and increase the likelihood that people will read it.
- <u>Emphasize value</u>: do not just use emails to explain the details of your business or the features of your offer. Instead, focus on how your product or service benefits users.
- <u>Create a sense of urgency</u>: make users feel that their next action can't wait. You can do this by offering exclusive offers with deadlines, such as a coupon code Due within a week.

- Include a Call to Action: Each of your emails should include a call-to-action that guides readers to your end goal. This should be presented as a prominent button with direct, action-oriented language such as *"Start Now"*, *"Grab It"*, *"Subscribe"* or *"Buy Now"*.
- Create anticipation: conclude your emails by increasing reader interest. Include a "P.S." to give hints about an upcoming offer, contest, brand new e-book and more.

5. Start the Campaign

Once you have created your emails, identified your target audience and goal, and refined your strategy, it is time to send them to users. Since the process is automated, simply set up the initial trigger (for example, a newsletter subscription) and specify the number of days between emails you want to run.

15°. What Are Google Ads and How Does it Works?

Google Ads is the advertising services platform of Google that allows all those who want to show ads in the results of the search engine and on its advertising network to do so strategically. Through data analysis and tools for refining the results it is possible to target potential customers who have shown interest in the brand. All this has a great benefit for advertisers: to reach the public in a targeted manner, allowing them to choose specific objectives for their ads, not to exceed the limit of advertising spending that had been set and consequently increasing the rate of return on investment in online marketing.

The functioning of the platform is based on 5 pillars:

- the approach to communication is friendly and conversational with the intention of creating a positive connection with the advertiser (human).
- Advertisers are reassured thanks to the awareness of the potential of the results that can be achieved (empowering).
- Google Ads communication is clear and direct, with few frills and a lot of respect for advertisers' time (direct).
- The reputation has been built over time through the transparency of operations (trustworthy).
- Reliability is the result of a continuous interchange between Google experts and advertisers (reliable).

The registration of the account on Google Ads is free, paid instead is the advertising that is conveyed through the platform. Advertisers can establish a budget and change it when necessary, they pay only when a customer performs an action such as clicking on the ad to visit the site or to contact the advertised activity by phone and they are not bound by any kind of contract, so they can pause or cancel the campaign at any time.

Google Ads does not require a minimum budget, but new advertisers are advised to start with an average budget of between 5 and 50 dollars per day in order to have a better chance of being published.

The system of Google Ads is based on the auction mechanism that sees on one hand the advertisers who want to publish their ads and on the other hand the Google Ads platform that wants to offer content relevant to the interests of its audience. Advertisers can create a campaign on their own by using the guided configuration procedure for the creation of ads or the online assistance service made available by Google. During the creation of the ad, words or phrases are set that correspond to the terms potentially used by users when searching for products or services such as those advertised. Keywords are matched to the ads created and whenever an ad is deemed suitable for a search, it can compete in the auction for publication. If the business to be promoted is hypothetically an auto repair center, the keyword might be "auto repair" matched to an ad promoting auto repair. If a user searches on Google using the phrase "car repair", the ad might appear in the paid search results of Google or on other car repair related websites. Among the various ads created for this search key, the platform ignores those that it considers unsuitable because they are directed to another country or not approved because they violate the publication rules. Instead, the ads that remain are selected according to several factors that Google Ads identifies in the bid set, the quality of the ad and the landing page, the qualitative thresholds of the ranking of the same, the user's search context (location, device, time, nature of search terms, other ads and search results displayed on the page and additional user attributes and indicators) and the expected impact of extensions and other ad formats. The auction mechanism is repeated for each Google search, so each auction may have different results from time to time depending on the competition at the time.

16°. Organization of The Account on Google Ads

At the definition of a campaign, there are ads that share different settings including budget, location targeting and distribution. Within an account it is possible to have multiple campaigns running, with ads in different locations and different budgets. The organization of the Google account is on three levels and understanding the relationship between them allows the advertiser to organize their work according to the audience segment they intend to target. The first level is that of the account to which is associated an email address, a password and unique billing information. The second level is that of the campaigns with customized settings applied to all the ads in the same campaign. The third one concerns the ad groups divided by similar keywords.

As far as campaigns are concerned, the settings available to the advertiser are:

- <u>campaign name</u>, which easily describes its theme and makes it easily identifiable within the account.
- <u>Campaign type</u>, whose configuration is adapted to the objectives that have been set.
- <u>Networks</u> in which you want to publish your ad according to the type of campaign chosen.
- <u>Devices</u> for customizing the ads.
- <u>Locations</u> chosen as the target, which must be consistent with the language and brand with which you address your customers.
- <u>Bids</u> that can be set manually and budget at the advertiser's discretion.
- <u>Extensions</u> to enhance the ad by providing more information.
- <u>Additional settings</u>, such as the ability to schedule the campaign.

<u>Text ads posted on the search network are composed of 3 elements:</u>

<u>the title text, the display URL, and the description text.</u>

1)The title text of an ad is the first thing that is noticed by users and is composed of three parts (title 1, title 2 and title 3, separated by a vertical bar), each of which must not exceed 30 characters. In this space, the advertiser must promote the product or service offered by including terms that users might enter within their Google searches.

2) The display URL is the part of the ad born from the combination of the final URL, the URL address of the website page that visitors will land on after clicking on the ad, and optional path fields that help those who see the ad understand where they will be redirected.

3) the description text is the space that the advertiser has available to insert details about the service or product he is promoting. Its maximum length is 90 characters.

17°. The 5 Essential Elements to Write an Effective Text Ad on Google Ads

A text ad on Google Ads is the opportunity for a company to make itself known online through a catchy title and a relevant description that links to the site of the product or service you are promoting. It is a handful of characters in which you are required to be specific and relevant, relevant, and engaging without losing the focus of the campaign, that is, convince the user to choose your ad among many. It is necessary to focus on what are the real advantages of your product or service. The user we intercept must be given a reason to choose our product over that of other competitors.

In the creation of a campaign on Google Ads, the advertiser has the possibility to choose whether to publish the ad within the search network - and thus make it appear, in response to a query, above the organic results marked by a specific label - or within the display network - and make it appear in the form of a banner while browsing different websites -. The communication approach varies for the two types of ads: if in the first case it is a pull approach, as the user asks and is provided with results relevant to his query, in the second case it is a push approach, as the ad appears while the user is browsing. The biggest difference between search and display ads is in the context in which they appear. If on the one hand we are dealing with someone who is actively looking for something we promote and we "only" must convince them to click on our ad instead of a competitor's one, on the other hand in the display network we intercept users who are browsing with intentions unknown to us. In search ads the content should focus not so much on what we are selling, but on why my offer is better than others, while in display ads we should also be able to interest or re-engage the user with what we are selling.

The ads must be unique and evocative, calling in the mind of the consumer images in which to identify and leveraging their conscious and latent needs, highlighting the immediate benefits of the offer. To effectively reach potential customers, text ads must meet the requirements of specificity and relevance and at the same time be interesting and engaging.

It is possible to identify 5 essential elements of writing effective text:

1) Include keywords in the ad text. The presence of keywords in the ad indicates the relevance of the ad with what users are looking for. If, for example, in promoting a wine shop's wine classes, the string "California wine" is included as a keyword, the ad title could be "Do you know California wine?". The creation of keyword lists requires the ability to identify with the user who will be searching for the products, knowledge of the field in which you operate if you decide to create ads for specific clients, but also resourcefulness in experimenting with generic keywords until you find the most effective ones.

2) Highlight what makes your service or product unique and authentic. Writing an ad that highlights the competitive advantage means answering the questions "what do we offer exclusively?", "what do we have exclusivity on?", "how long have we been on the market?" and using words that leverage the concepts of uniqueness, exclusivity, and longevity, respectively. So, if the store that will be sponsored by the ad is the official dealer of a given product in an area, it is good to focus on this aspect. Similarly, if the presence on the market for a long time is synonymous with a guarantee of quality, it is precisely on this aspect that the advertiser should direct the writing of the texts. All this, of course, in the light of the objectives that have been set and without distorting the communication style of the brand.

3) Include information about prices, promotions, and exclusive offers. The text ads present within the Google search network are often displayed while the user is in the process of deciding on a purchase or an action to be taken. Inside the announcement it is good then to insert all the elements that help him to decide and that favor his transformation from user to customer. Prices, promotions and exclusive offers can represent a competitive advantage, but also words like "new" or "download" represent immediate advantages that make the user curious or satisfy his need for concreteness.

4) Focus your text on the benefits of your product or service. Always to meet the users' need for concreteness, it is always better to focus on the benefits that the sponsored product or service can bring compared to the functions that characterize it.

5) Consistency between landing page and landing page ad. Ads are meant to showcase the immediate benefits of the offer they are promoting, and these benefits must also be found within the landing page they are linked to. If users do not find what they were promised in the ad, they may leave the site and negatively memorize the brand that "tricked" them, so it is extremely important to always verify that the promotions and products mentioned are present on the landing page.

Perry Marshall, a famous American online marketing consultant, is among the most authoritative sources when it comes to online marketing. Marshall illustrates a surprising technique in its effectiveness to optimize the performance of a pay per click campaign: it is the so-called "Peel & Stick". Starting from the analysis of the most performing keywords for each group of ads, Marshall suggests moving them to a specific group, built ad hoc around a single keyword, and accompanying it with an ad that perfectly matches the keyword (and maybe even contains it in the title). It is a sort of "click and stick" that can significantly maximize the CTR by increasing the percentage of users who click on an ad after reading its title. CTR (click through rate) is a % value that represents the ratio between the total number of impressions, i.e., the number of times the ad was viewed, and the clicks on the ad link. On average, a sufficient through ctr does not fall below 2% and aiming to increase its value, in this specific case, is the purpose of an optimization. Each Google Ads campaign is a story in itself, it is true, but Perry Marshall identifies a number of best practices that undoubtedly contribute significantly to improving performance and results obtained through Google Ads. Among these: the scheduling of ads to manage the timing of the publication; geotargeting to focus the budget on specific areas of interest; the use of bidding strategies differentiated by device; the drafting of a list of negative keywords that keeps the ads away from misleading thematic or semantic combinations or simply not in line with the target audience.

18°. How to Create A Video Campaign on Google Ads?

How to Create A Video Campaign on Google Ads?

Video campaigns represent a type of campaign present on Google Ads that allows you to show stand-alone video ads or insert them in streaming on YouTube or Google's display network.

Among the available video formats there are:

- <u>Ignorable in-stream ads</u>, which are played before, during or after other videos and for which the viewer is asked whether or not to ignore them after viewing the first 5 seconds.
- <u>In-stream, non-ignored ads</u>, which last up to 15 seconds and are designed to reach customers with the entire video message.
- <u>Discovery video ads</u>, which reach users while they are intent on discovering other content on YouTube.
- <u>Outstream ads</u>, which run on partner sites and initially play with sound turned off.
- <u>Bumper ads</u>, short-form video ads with punchy, memorable messages.

There is also the masthead ad format, which is only available by reservation with a Google sales consultant, which allows you to reach an exceptionally large audience in a short period of time.

Analyze the Performance of a Campaign on Google Ads

Data about the coverage of a campaign is displayed within the Google Ads statistics table. A campaign's unique coverage metrics measure the total number of users who were shown an ad and allow the advertiser to understand how many times users viewed the ad. These include unique users and average frequency of impressions per user (also available for 7- and 30-day intervals)

As far as the performance of a campaign is concerned, it is possible to find summary sheets with a line graph in the "Overview" of Google Ads. The consultation of specific performance data is customizable with columns, segments and filters that allow a practical overview of the data and the creation of downloadable and shareable reports.

19° What Are Google Ads Extensions and How to Use Them?

Google Ads extensions are a feature offered by the online advertising service and allow you to insert additional information within the advertisement. Thanks to the extensions you can add to your advertisement some specifics about a particular topic that can be extremely useful to the user who performs a keyword search. The implementation of Google Ads extensions within the campaigns is fundamental, moreover, for the Page Rank, that is the level of "popularity" assigned by Google to individual Web pages. There are different types of extensions. I will list them below going into the merits to explain the functionality.

- **<u>Sitelink Extensions.</u>**
- **<u>Callout Extension.</u>**
- **<u>Structured Snippet Extensions.</u>**
- **<u>Call Extensions.</u>**
- **<u>Message Extensions.</u>**
- **<u>Location Extensions.</u>**
- **<u>Price Extensions.</u>**
- **<u>App Extensions.</u>**
- **<u>Promotion Extensions.</u>**
- **<u>Automated ad Extensions.</u>**

<u>Sitelink Extensions</u> allow to add to the ad other specific pages of our site. It is important to consider that the URL of the sitelink must be different from the final URL of our ad to avoid possible problems of publication by Google.

<u>Callout Extension</u> is represented by an additional line placed right after the ad containing information about particular aspects of the advertised product or service. Callouts can be from 1 to 4 and are separated by dots.

<u>Structured Snippet Extensions</u> are "an evolution" of callouts because they describe the characteristics of the products or services shown in the ads in depth to provide a clear and complete vision to the user who performs a search. The structured snippets displayed will be no more than two at a time, depending on Google's calculations.

Call Extensions are especially useful and show the phone number of the business being advertised next to the website address and from mobile. By clicking, you can immediately place the call.

Message Extensions, like Call Extensions allow you to contact the business directly, avoiding having to call or enter the site and fill out any forms. Next to the ad will be placed a SMS icon that will allow you to write a text message saving time!

Location Extensions are extremely useful to indicate the address of the activity and associate it to a map to make it easy to reach the physical location that provides the service or sells the product indicated in the ad. If you want to have the possibility to activate this type of extension, you will need to connect your AdWords account to Google My Business.

Price Extensions allow you to insert (from 3 to 8) the prices of products and services to advertise exclusively the brand and the offer you want to focus the user's attention on. This type of extension is only available for search network campaigns and are placed under the advertisement.

App Extensions allow you to redirect to the app page or start downloading it. AdWords will show the ad only to those who are interested in apps dedicated to the Android operating system (if in possession of an Android device) and to iOS (if in possession of an Apple device).

Promotion Extensions are indicated in the ad in bold and indicate a particular promotion linked to an event or holiday. These extensions allow the advertiser to attract potential customers looking for specific discounts and, by clicking on them, you will be directed to the page dedicated to the special offer.

Automated ad Extensions are generated by AdWords to improve ad performance and do not need to be set up. Automated ad extensions can still be disabled if they are not needed or if they do not make improvements to the ads.

<u>How to set up Google Ads extensions?</u>

Once you log into Google Ads, use the following sequence to set up extensions:

1. Select your campaign or ad group.

2. Click the "Ads & Extensions" tab on the left, the "Extensions" tab across the top, and then the large + sign to create a new extension.

3. From the drop-down menu that appears, select the extension you want to create (hovering over each extension will show a brief description of what it does). Customize each type of extension you wish to set up (Google will provide a preview of your ad as you create it) and then click save. Google offers both manual and automated extensions.

20°. Tools to Optimize A Campaign on Google Ads

Tests and experiments are techniques widely used in the world of online marketing, to optimize web page, increase the performance of a site or conversion rates of advertising campaigns but especially of ecommerce.

<u>AB Testing</u> is one of the most useful tools for this purpose and is among the best known and appreciated strategies. A/B testing is an experiment whereby we can administer two different versions (version A and version B, or "original" and "variant") of a web page, an advertisement, a title, a photo, a form, a button, or any element we want to test to an audience we define. Thanks to these tests, we will show a percentage of users the original version and another percentage of users the variant, and we will measure the effects.

But what exactly does this concept consist of and how do you implement one properly?

Let us see together the main characteristics of an effective AB test and some ideas to realize it. The moment you publish a website, put a landing page online or start an advertising campaign is just the beginning of an indispensable process of monitoring results and experiments aimed at optimizing the performance of the work done. The possibility of improving the performance is what pushes to put in place specific tests, including AB testing, also called <u>AB Test or A/B Split Testing</u>. This is a system aimed at understanding how the audience reacts to what is being proposed to them, by administering multiple versions of a piece of content, such as the same ad, the same page or the same title, image, or button. Understanding what the audience thinks of what is being offered is essential to understand what works and what does not, what is best received and what, when put to the test, offers the best performance. The results of such tests should be carefully recorded as numbers, percentages, and data, analyzed carefully and then used to build a valid online product optimization. To optimize a campaign on Google Ads, it is extremely helpful to use tools to improve the performance of the campaigns.

I believe that <u>SplitTester</u>, designed by Perry Marshall, can certainly be of help. It is a tool to effectively manage A/B tests. By entering the number of clicks and the CTR of both ads, the tool can predict which ad will produce better results in the long run, whether it is worth waiting for the natural timing of the A/B test or whether there are low chances of getting appreciable results.

Another useful tool for A/B Testing is <u>A/B Test Significance Calculator</u>, it provides precise information about the level of reliability of a test starting from the input of some key variables, such as the number of visitors or conversions of a website or landing page.

Equally useful are the tools for finding new keywords: among them is <u>ÜberSuggest</u>, which can generate an immense number of keywords from a first search key.

These are just some of the tools you can use. This is just a small indicative list to give you a first selection and to guide you in your research. There are a lot of Tools and as I want to point out I always leave to you the choice on which tool is the best for you for your specific needs.

21°. Is Facebook Ads an Outdated Sponsorship Method?

Although there are other extraordinarily strong platforms like Instagram or TikTok, Facebook is still a winning platform to make sponsored campaigns for your affiliate links.

There are about 2.60 billion registered users on Facebook. Of these, about 1.75 billion users access their profile daily, meaning they use this social network every day (they are therefore "active users") and 96% of these prefer to access from mobile devices, such as smartphones. An active user, on average, spends on social networks 2 hours and a half per day. If we consider the hours of free time and set aside 8 hours of sleep and 8 hours of work or study, that is not a small amount at all. So, <u>93% of marketers extensively use Facebook ads</u>, because among all forms of advertising, <u>it is the one that has the best return on investment</u>. The Facebook ads system is in fact one of the main tools that web marketers have at their disposal. I say main because it is a very well tested system, with a clear and effective management panel, with many interesting features and above all relatively cheap compared to other systems.

I want to give you some tips on how to optimize a campaign on Facebook.

Optimizing Schedules

The advertising activity, like all activities of modern marketing, must keep at the center of strategic choices the user, always.

Therefore, in the creation of a campaign, we should not only keep in mind the type of language, message, and effective levers for our target audience, but also the times in which it is most likely to consult an ad in terms of time. Quite simply, if our target audience is most likely an employee and what we want to offer them requires enough time for consultation/registration, running the ad during office hours is probably not the right move. The Facebook system, as well as other ad systems, also allows us to activate the campaign only during certain time slots. In this case it might be interesting to test the pre-office interval and/or lunch break and/or post office.

<u>Age Optimization</u>

A further optimization test can be implemented by segmenting our audience by age. In fact, the Facebook ad dashboard allows us to go into great detail about performance and we can also appreciate ad performance for each age group that makes up the audience we have selected.

<u>Optimization by Positioning</u>

Positioning means where the ad will appear. We have a macro division at desktop and mobile level and for each of them Facebook then proposes different types of ads including home feed, in-stream video, stories, Instagram home feed, Instagram stories, Audience Network (= other Facebook partner sites) or Messenger.

I recommend you also use the <u>Audience Insights</u> tool, made available by Facebook, it allows you to analyze your target audience, both as a composition and as behaviors (clicks, interactions etc..).

A useful tool that allows you to understand the slice of the market you are targeting.

You can understand, in fact, how many Facebook users have interest in your niche market, if they click a little or a lot, what age they are and so on. Audience Insights is great because it gives you an idea of what to expect from your Facebook audience. Facebook is a platform with unlimited customer potential. By putting in place well thought out strategies and techniques, it can turn into a profitable source of traffic, making you really high money.

Here are ways to pay for your Facebook ads:

- <u>Per impression.</u> You pay for each display of the ad. This mode is recommended for campaigns that aim at brand consolidation.
- <u>Per click.</u> You pay only when users click on the ad. Useful when there is a specific CTA that leads to a landing page or website.
- <u>Per action.</u> In this case you pay only if the user performs an action such as filling out a contact form or making a purchase.

By choosing between these options, you direct Facebook's algorithm to suggest your ads to people who are likely to take certain actions. Thus, you increase the conversion rate.

It is only fair, however, to remember that it takes time to get the first meaningful results. In particular, if you are just starting out with Facebook ads, the advice is to be patient and don't give up after the first few days.

22°. Why Advertise on Instagram?

In the path to climbing the business ladder, a great thing is to always try to understand where the best opportunities are, where to find the pond most full of fish and consequently where to go fishing for them. Try to monetize as much as possible by looking for the best channels to launch affiliate marketing content and links.

Definitely one area to focus on is Instagram.

Instagram has reached the figure of over 700 million active users worldwide, a figure that has been confirmed by Mark Zuckerberg himself on his Facebook profile. According to a recent analysis by Locowise, Instagram would have an interaction rate (engagement rate) 70% higher than Facebook. Interactions are defined as any action the user does with a post: like, comment, purchase, site visit and so on. This is certainly one of the main reasons why it is worth promoting your products/services on this Social Network. Provided that the product/service and the type of advertising campaign is in line with the target users present on Instagram. Never forget that every brand must have an exact study and analysis of the end user to whom it is addressed.

Before proceeding with any other action, it is important to do a thorough research on your competitors. Research those who are the leaders in the industry you want to "attack" and analyze their Ads campaigns, what call-to-actions they use and how many interactions they manage to generate. One piece of advice I can give you is to use some strategy. It is actually simpler than you might think. Many, if not all, people use the Facebook pixel for remarketing. In short, it is a way to track users who have been to a particular site and then repost sponsored posts to them. Now that you know a little more about how your competition moves on Instagram, it is time to determine the primary focus of your Instagram ad campaign.

Crucial question: what do you want people to do when they view your sponsored post?

Instagram ADS uses the same platform as Facebook, and there are multiple goals that can be chosen:

Brand awareness: increase your brand awareness.

Coverage: show your ad to the maximum number of people (ideal for ads related to important news).

Traffic: increase clicks to your website or to your App on the App Store or Google Play.

Interaction: engage users as much as possible to take an action on your post such as likes, shares, events, comments, or purchases.

App installs: land users in the store where your app is and entice them to download.

Video views: promote your videos and get more views.

Conversions: push people to take actions on a site or app, such as making a purchase.

One of the most obvious strengths of advertising on Instagram is precisely the targeting of the audience as it can be processed according to different aspects, including behavioral.

Instagram Ads offers a wide choice as with Facebook Ads, including targeting according to location, gender, interests, and behavior.

In the area of targeting on Instagram & Facebook ads, it is worth mentioning the "Lookalike Audience". An effective tool that manages to create a super specific audience for your sponsored post. Similar audiences tend to convert more because people have a genuine interest in that specific industry/product/service.

The last step, to create a sponsored post that works on Instagram you need to unleash your creativity. Make something that is cool. Do not do something that is mundane and standard like everyone else. Be original and differentiate yourself. Make the user while scrolling through photos on Instagram be struck by your ad and stop to look at it.

There are several different types of creative for Instagram Ads:

- Single image or with multiple images to scroll through a post.

- Single Video: a post with video.
- Slideshow: a post with continuous looping video (max 10 images).
- Canvas: a post where you can tell a story by combining images and video.

The choice is dictated by the message you want to give and the goal you want to achieve.

Based on my experience, I can say that videos compared to images brought me more encouraging results, but it could simply be because it was the most suitable format for the type of campaign I was running.

23°. Why Tiktok Could Be A Super Boost for Your Business?

What Is TikTok?; How Long Can TikTok Videos Be?; Tiktok Advertising: Can We Advertise on TikTok?; Which Are the Different Types of Tik Tok Ads?; How Much Does It Cost to Advertise on Tiktok?;

I personally think that TikTok, given the ever-growing numbers, is an extremely interesting platform to boost our business in the world of affiliate marketing.

From the first moment it was launched in 2017, Tiktok is growing in popularity day by day and in a noticeably short time it has become one of the most used social media platforms worldwide, surpassing competitors like Snapchat. With this huge number of users, it seems more and more obvious for social media marketers to invest in this new platform.

By now, TikTok has over 1 billion users worldwide and around 40 million daily active users. It is definitely under the eye of the storm for its number of daily active users.

However, before you consider starting an ad campaign on TikTok, you need to get to know it better.

<u>Who (I'm mostly referring to age in this case) uses Tiktok the most?</u>

<u>How much do ads cost?</u>

<u>How to advertise on TikTok?</u>

The answers to these kinds of questions would help you decide whether or not you should consider it as a marketing platform for your business.

What is TikTok?

TikTok is mainly a video sharing app launched in early 2017 by Chinese developer ByteDance. Later, the owner decided that he wanted to buy the well-known app Musicall.ly, which was becoming immensely popular at that time. ByteDance bought Musical.ly on November 9, 2017 and combined the two apps into one app called TikTok on August 2, 2018. This is how these two popular video sharing apps were converted into one and the audience was also integrated. You do not need to follow anyone on TikTok in order to watch videos. All you have to do is open the app and start scrolling through the videos that are offered one after the other. You can also search for videos on your favorite topics using the relevant hashtags.

How Long Can TikTok Videos Be?

Individual TikTok videos are 15 seconds long, but there is an option to post longer videos by putting several clips together up to 60 seconds. Another thing to remember is that accounts over 1000 followers can post longer videos.

Who Primarily Uses TikTok?

TikTok, as well as its sister app Musical.ly, is mainly used by teenagers.

There are many interesting statistics according to the accurate reports that the website "Marketing chart" has provided in a chart. According to their website, the average age of Tiktok users is 18-24 (3.7 million), which represents just over a quarter (25.8%) of the total adult visitors in the United States. Another quarter (24.5%) of visitors aged 18 and older were in the 25-34 age group. TikTok is used by 2 million more women (8.2 million) than men (6.1 million), and its reach is highest among women ages 18-24 (14.9% adoption).

So, if you are thinking about leveraging Tik Tok ads, keep in mind that your audience is, on average, 18 to 30 years old.

Tiktok Advertising: Can We Advertise on TikTok?

On February 21, 2019, TikTok announced the opening of the platform to advertisements, attracting the attention of all social media managers. So, it's obvious that we can all advertise on TikTok now, but first you need to make sure that your business has the necessary requirements to start a campaign. Below we outline the factors that can help you decide whether TikTok is suitable for your business or not.

The Target Audience

The results from Tik Tok campaigns depend heavily on who your target audience is. If you have an adult audience and offer services related to, for example, bank accounts or hosting platforms, TikTok might not be the right place for you. But if you have a youth-friendly business, you should definitely give it a try as 66% of TikTok users are under 30 years old. So, it would be a great investment.

Visual Content

To be successful on TikTok you need to have a good amount of quality visual content to share. Your company needs to create videos that can represent your brand or product in a way that TikTokers would accept. This is because TikTok is primarily about sharing videos. So, if you have the ability to create the right content to stand out on TikTok, don't hesitate and get started.

Budget

Tik Tok ads are new to the industry, in fact there are still very few and rare ads on the platform. Small businesses are still hard to find on Tiktok and larger companies such as Nike, Disney, and Grubhub, are the ones that have made their way there first. Currently, the cost of ads is the most expensive compared to all other social media.

Target

The next step is to set the target audience to view your ads. You can set your target audience by geographic area, age, gender, language, interests, devices, and more.

Choose the Budget and Plan the Ad

We have reached the section where you need to define exactly the amount you will pay for the ad and the time and date when the ad will run.

Set the Goal of The Ad Campaign

The objective of the campaign determines the goals you wish to achieve with the ads you run. The options to choose from are: Conversion, Clicks or Impressions (as we have seen before for other social networks) and your bids will be optimized according to the selected goal. Another thing you can set on this page is deciding whether you want to set up conversion tracking for app installs or certain elements of your landing page via pixels.

<u>Ad</u>

Since we have almost reached the end of creating an ad, it is time to customize your ad and design how you want it to display. TikTok ads can be video, horizontal, vertical, or square images.

Another unique advertising option that Tiktok offers its users is an interesting creation tool called "<u>Video Creation Kit</u>".

<u>Which Are the Different Types of Tik Tok Ads?</u>

<u>Acquisition</u>

Acquisition ads are the ads that appear immediately after a user opens TikTok. Takeovers include external or internal links that can redirect a user to other TikTok accounts or videos or a website on the Internet.

Note: Only one advertiser per day may use this type of ad on TikTok.

<u>Native Video Ads</u>

Native video ads are placed at the bottom of a TikTok video or inserted at the end of the video. These ads will be directed to your website or app. Native video ads are cheaper than acquisition ads.

<u>Hashtag Video Challenges</u>

TikTokers love to take on challenges and tackle them in their own style, so it would be an incredibly wise idea to accompany videos with the hashtag of the hottest trend of the moment.

<u>How Much Does It Cost to Advertise on Tiktok?</u>

Tik Tok ads, as mentioned above, are more expensive than any other social media ad because they are new and rare and consequently also more efficient, costs start at an average of $10 per CPM and can go up to $300,000 as the ad campaign gets bigger.

<u>How to Advertise on TikTok?</u>

Sign up for a Tik Tok ad account. The Tiktok advertising platform is separate from a Tiktok account and profile. So the first step in creating a Tik Tok ad is to go to the Tik Tok ads page and sign in so you can start your ad campaign. If you do not have an ad account yet, create one.

<u>Create your ad campaign.</u>

After registering for the ad account campaign, you will be provided with a dashboard where you can draft new ads and keep track of ad campaigns.

To create your first Tik Tok ad, proceed as follows:

Go to the Tik Tok ad dashboard.

Click on the "campaign tab" at the top of the page.

Click on the Create button.

Choose a campaign goal (traffic, conversions, or app install).

Next, set a name for your campaign.

Define the campaign budget (Daily Budget or Total Budget option).

Note: the minimum budget amount must be $500 for both Daily Budget and Total Budget.

Define positions and ad targeting.

Positions: in this step, you can set the position in which to display Tik Tok ads. Do you want them to be placed between Tiktoker stories or do you want them to appear in TikTok's video feed? Or you can simply let the platform decide where to place your ads.

24°. Performance Marketing Metrics

I think it is appropriate to go into the merits of some metrics that are especially important to know and that serve as a reference to understand whether your advertising campaign is working well or not. It is important, since you invest money for sponsorships, that these are the most performing as possible, consequently that the money invested gives you the maximum in terms of economic return.

Analyze serves to understand if you are operating in gain, in loss or in break-even. If you are in profit you can assume to leave it like that because the campaign is correctly set, or you can think about increasing the investment to push even more and assume to earn even more, if you understand that there is a positive trend. If, on the other hand, a campaign is negative you can think about making corrective maneuvers and if, once done, there are no improvements you can abandon the campaign because it is uneconomic. It is especially important to monitor your campaign daily, to understand if you are proceeding in the right direction, if you have to make corrections in progress. It is necessary to observe which keywords are most searched and understand if it can be useful or not to increase or decrease the amount to spend for each click. In practice you will be in a control cabin and you must monitor the charts and in general the performance of your work since you are investing your money and the goal is always to maximize. No one can have a crystal ball and there are no standard solutions. You need to start campaigning first, maybe start with low initial budgets if you are just starting out and do not have much experience, just to experiment. For example, you could start with a budget set at 0.40 cents per click for each keyword, with 0.60 cents for the 10 keywords that you consider most important or related to your product or service that you are going to sponsor. Then over time you can increase the amounts of your sponsorships and if your business is structured and important, you can also invest $ 100,000 per month with a return of $ 120,000 or more.

Everything is always scalable and gradual over time. Remember, this business has no limits, and you do not have to limit yourself either. The wise saying "*Don't put a roof over your head*" always applies.

Click-through Rate (Click and open rate)

Through the click-through rate it is possible to measure the number of clicks on a call to action or on a specific link. Starting from this data, obtained through a tracking system, it is possible to obtain two important pieces of information: the actual effectiveness of a campaign and the origin of the clicks. The latter is extremely useful since, acting in real time, it is possible to redefine the most strategically effective channels.

The click-through rate is also the metric that allows the advertiser to quantify the rate he will pay in pay per click campaigns.

Conversion Rate

Once the open rate has been defined, through the conversion rate it is possible to measure the conversion rates per requested action and therefore monitor the number of subscriptions to a newsletter, the number of downloads or the number of subscriptions following the completion of a form. Based on the objective of the campaign is possible to define through the conversion rate the most appropriate payment model, such as the cost per lead (CPL) and the cost per action or cost per acquisition (CPA).

Social Metrics

Monitoring social media performance is necessary to understand the online activity of your users and obtain, through social media monitoring tools, important information to refine your business strategy. Again, monitoring performance in real time allows you to take immediate action and consistently replicate actions that have been successful and contributed to a virtuous performance.

Post Visualization

The number of views of a post is a metric that allows to understand how much a content is of interest for its target. Its monitoring allows a targeted and effective planning, oriented to increase the number of visits and declined on the basis of the trending topics of the reference sector.

25°. How Important Is It to Analyze Data? What Is Digital Analysis?

Digital analysis is the analysis of qualitative and quantitative data about your company and your competitors in order to achieve a continuous improvement of the online experience that your users can have and to push them towards the desired results (both online and offline). Starting from this concept, it is possible to consider the fundamental theme in digital marketing today and that is the importance of implementing "customer-centric" strategies.

A customer can begin their journey to purchase at any time and place; therefore, a marketer's job is to predict where and when customers will come in and what messages they need to read. Analytics is an integral part of this process, and interpreting data is key to making decisions about what you need to do online to understand and connect with customers. The internet is constantly changing and evolving, a fact that is now well known, but are you taking advantage of these changes?

Not only do businesses need a website, but they need a company blog and social media profiles including Facebook, Twitter, and Instagram. To professionally manage all these pieces, you need, then, proper planning, goals and reporting. Companies need to look at both quantitative and qualitative data, measure results and implement a continuous improvement process. This work may seem huge and impossible and will undoubtedly take time, but with the web becoming the first point of contact for any customer, it is critical to know the data to be successful.

Digital analytics is a key aspect of any online business for so many reasons; the main one involves making decisions that are "smart" and thoughtful based on data history. One tool that can definitely help you in the data analysis process is Google Analytics. According to Google, about 90% of the world's websites have Google Analytics installed as their measurement software, but surprisingly only 30% log in to evaluate their data. As you can imagine, even though it is a freemium software, most of the features of the completely free version of Google Analytics allow a detailed analysis of several aspects that are functional to the understanding of the performance trend, namely:

- mode of user acquisition
- user behavior on the site
- monitoring of objectives (and conversions).

Before proceeding with the analysis of the platform settings it is necessary to make a brief distinction between micro and macro conversions: a conversion is an action that you want users to perform on a website (or a mobile app) as it brings value (actual or potential) to the business. When the action is actual, we talk about macro-conversion, when it is potential, we talk about micro-conversion.

Some practical examples can undoubtedly clarify ideas. Suppose we must define the micro-conversions of an eCommerce of customizable t-shirts and hats; in this case the macro-conversions that users can make are:

- buy one or more hats and/or sweatshirts.

However, there may be actions that do not have immediate value, but that can be transformed in the short or long term in macro-conversions. Think for example of:

- requests for quotes of higher quantities
- newsletter subscriptions to join special discounts and offers.

Obviously, this is just an example, however typical of a <u>B2C</u> context, or <u>Business to Consumer</u> with implementation of eCommerce platform.

In the case of a <u>B2B</u> or <u>Business to Business</u>, in fact, they can be considered to all effects macro-conversions actions such as the following:

- request for quote
- request for a demo (in the case of software, for example)
- telephone calls.

The micro-conversions, instead, could be:

- visualizations of specific product/service pages (such as landing pages summarizing all specifications)
- video demo views.

In conclusion, analyze and monitor your journey. Every business is based on numbers. Like any business or like managing your personal finances you have to be good at increasing revenue and reducing costs. As you buy a product on offer at the supermarket, with a 30% discount, you have to do the same with your campaigns, if on the one hand you have to optimize costs, on the other hand you have to make sure that if you spend to make advertising, that at least this expenditure is optimized with the best possible result in terms of sales or conversions, according to the initial and strategic objectives that you have set.

26° How Does Ad-Blocking Negatively Affect Affiliate Marketing?

When we talk about Affiliate Marketing we cannot not talk, for completeness, also about the phenomenon of ad-blockers. Since in order to sell, you will surely have to advertise your products, your affiliate links, your content, ad-blocking could be slowing you down in pursuing your goals. For the sake of completeness, it is only fair that I also inform you about this aspect present on the web. By ad blocker or ad blocking, we mean a technology that is useful in preventing the display or download of advertising, allowing visitors to a website to enjoy content without any type of advertisement.

The ad-blocker phenomenon has become pervasive globally, posing significant challenges to content sites, brands, marketing agencies and tech providers. Emerging data indicates that ad-blocking is indeed becoming a problem and a major obstacle for everyone in the marketing world and their client brands.

How Many People Are Using Ad-Blocking?

According to PageFair and Adobe in 2015 there were about 198 million users worldwide already blocking ads. In 2016, the number grew by 41% globally, while the growth rate in the U.S. was 48%. All of this was costing publishers a whopping $22 billion. What about today? By 2021, at least 34% of adults 18 and older are actively using ad-blockers. The average user is male, computer savvy and has minor children in their household.

Which Are the Ads That Encourage the Use of Ad-Blockers?

Visitors have been driven to adopt ad-blockers primarily because of three types of unwanted ad formats:

1. Videos that play automatically.

2. Invasive ads that interrupt browsing.

3. Flashing banners.

Interestingly, the growing use of ad-blockers is not only motivated by a widespread 'dislike' of ads, but specifically relates to the methods of publication.

Three of the main reasons why users start using ad-blockers are:

- Advertising negatively affects the performance of the device.
- Device gets attacked by viruses and malware.
- Growing awareness about available ad-blocking technologies.

The main reason people continue to use ad-blockers then, has more to do with protecting their device than avoiding the advertising itself. More and more people are concerned about protecting their computers, tablets and smartphones from viruses and malware, while trying to increase the performance of their devices. Thus, there is a negative sentiment towards the advertising that one is forced to see, and many users feel that it distracts them too much from what they are doing. However, if advertising translated into better access to content, many users would probably disable their ad-blocker right away.

The Number of Users Using Ad-Blocking Is Growing.

Surely most people do not realize that advertising allows to finance the fruition of a content, even digital. They are unaware of this role: it is in fact to all intents and purposes the tool that allows free access to our favorite sites. The frustration generated by advertising in its current form is the driving force behind the increased adoption rates of ad-blockers globally.

Accessing online content has become increasingly difficult due to the amount of advertising that needs to be displayed before getting to what a user started browsing for. The vast improvement in technology has in a way contributed to an even more frustrating user experience on so many websites, regardless of loading times, connection speed etc. Slower loading times and higher data consumption on mobile devices have been the main reasons behind the use of ad-blockers in areas like Indonesia. In short, for some, advertising is considered unnecessary, intrusive, and irrelevant. In particular, the spread of mobile devices has only increased the use of ad blockers. In fact, recent research indicates that one in three smartphone owners feels they see too many ads while browsing the Internet via mobile. In reality, most users are still unaware that ad blocking technology is also available via mobile. Once this awareness increases, the advertising industry can expect another big drop in revenue.

Affiliate marketing is able to deliver value through its data-tracking capabilities, providing product information, pricing, reviews, discount codes or cashback, with the goal of encouraging a user to purchase. The affiliate site is paid a commission on all sales generated through customer conversion; this exchange results in a mutually beneficial and transparent partnership. Any domain that performs display activity or uses affiliation may be blacklisted by ad blockers. This means that banners are not displayed, click-throughs fail, and tracking may not load properly on the advertiser's site. The consequence is greater difficulty in tracking sales and rewarding publishers.

The Role of Browsers

Even "biggies" like Google, Apple and Microsoft are taking a stand and have taken the field. In February 2018, Chrome released an already built-in ad-blocker by default, which to date has over 60 million users. This development is significant as Chrome is currently used to view about 56% of web pages, according to analysis provided by StatCounter. Chrome has reported that about 42% of websites have reduced advertising practices deemed unacceptable in order to meet Google's standards.

As part of the process, Google evaluates websites and sends alerts to sites with overly intrusive ads. If the site fails to change its activity, it is added to a blacklist. Once blacklisted, Chrome blocks all ads until the site comes back into compliance with Chrome's standards.

Advertisers and The Buying and Selling of Advertising Space

In advertising, as in many other areas, money is king. It is therefore not surprising that advertisers and all ad buyers in general must and can play a key role in driving change.

However, it is also likely that there will be renewed controversy over the proposal to adopt a selective ad-blocking "philosophy," even though this is surely the most effective method at the moment to convince sites to comply.

The Current State

Undoubtedly, online advertising has contributed to the growth of the Internet, even funding platforms like Facebook and Google, without forcing the public to pay to enjoy the content. Just on Facebook, advertising exploded unleashing a digital phenomenon that has grown on a large scale. Now, by blocking these annoying and intrusive advertisements, readers are about to discover the true cost of all those websites they used to visit for free. We are seeing more and more content sites starting to offer subscription models or paywalls on site to encourage donations to keep their pages active.

Will Publishers Start Offering Subscription-Based Subscription Models?

All publishers are exploring a range of options designed to help them cope with the continued rise of ad-blockers and their negative impact on the revenue usually generated through online advertising. The New York Times and Washington Post have followed the Wall Street Journal's lead and implemented "paywalls" within their content, making it premium and only available for a small fee to gain access to membership.

Wired initially decided to block readers who had ad-blockers active, while online news site Salon tried to allow ad blockers on the condition that users agreed to an exchange: access to their browsers to mine cryptocurrencies (a form of digital currency that is difficult to counterfeit).

Surely, the future is to find a solution that can be as reasonable as possible, which on the one hand protects consumers from continued exposure to aggressive advertising, but on the other hand will try to protect the market related to paid content advertising because it is too important a market. Most likely it will come down to encouraging more users to implement unlocks in exchange for content, a kind of exchange and use a little more conscious and active, rather than passive advertising. A sort of more ethical use of content on the web. A path certainly not short, but certainly desirable

Final Considerations

We have come to my final thoughts. Thoughts that I want to share with you, after analyzing many aspects of affiliate marketing.

At the beginning the enthusiasm is sky high, after all it is normal and it is good to be optimistic, affiliate marketing is a fantastic world, unfortunately however, most people do not actually succeed in realizing their dreams.

Many of the reasons I am going to list may seem obvious or repetitive, but often we do not give them the right importance.

Trust me when I say that the secret to success lies in these points, the rest will follow.

Personally, I started to get results in this field only when I was definitely convinced of the points that we will see shortly, until then I had wasted my time in vain.

<u>1. Get rid of excuses and pretexts.</u>

Excuses are one of the worst anchors that can drown you in the abyss. People, past their initial enthusiasm, start making excuses even before they start.

Here are some recurring examples:

- I am not a programmer, and I do not know anything about web design.
- It takes too much time that I do not have.
- There is too much competition.
- Most people fail in this area.
- I do not have enough money.

From personal experience, I have seen the most unlikely people succeed in this field. People with no college degree, no special skills or experience, just a lot of passion and willpower. Remember just one thing: most of the people who are succeeding in this field were initially in a worse position than you are.

<u>Do not waste your time contemplating all the possible problems but use</u>

that time to find solutions.

One thought I always carry within me that gives me the right motivation is this:

If someone else has succeeded, I can succeed.

2. Failing and losing money.

Here is the second major obstacle.

Many people are not suited for business, this is because they have too low a "fear threshold". They are constantly afraid of failing, afraid of losing money. I cannot blame those who are afraid, only, it is necessary to clarify this point.

All the greatest businesses in the world are based on risk and overcoming these fears, otherwise none of them would ever exist.

But let us stop for a moment and analyze the real, modern world:

Think about how many people every day, after spending thousands of dollars on college studies, later find themselves doing underpaid work?

Think about those people who open a restaurant and take out several loans from the bank and then find themselves working 16 hours a day just to pay off all their debts.

How much money is lost on those occasions or any other entrepreneurial activity with huge initial costs?

Well, compared to the real world, to what it might cost to open any activity in the city center for example, affiliate marketing is a ridiculous investment.

How can you expect to be successful while being afraid to invest even a few hundred dollars?

3. Only successful campaigns count.

It does not matter how many times you fail, only the times you succeed.

What do I mean by this?

Most people focus primarily on how many campaigns have failed. By working this way, you drastically decrease your chances of success and lose all enthusiasm.

The trick lies in always being focused on the goal and finding your winning campaign.

4. Stop thinking and act.

The mind travels at a far greater speed than the body. Just think of the handwriting slower than the thought formulating in the mind. Often people spend most of their time thinking, evaluating, planning, and studying without ever taking action. Many end up getting tired before they even start. The fear is to start off on the wrong foot.

We continually search the web in hopes of finding the ultimate foolproof trick that will allow us to earn money easily and without risk. The truth is this trick does not exist and anyone who tells you otherwise is lying.

The only way to understand exactly how to behave in order to succeed with affiliate marketing, is to act in first person and test on your own skin all the possible strategies designed according to your goal to be achieved.

Succeeding with a campaign is a skill, and like all skills it takes practice.

You will learn a lot more by spending $500 on a campaign than you will in a year of study. Do not worry if your techniques fail at first, everyone who has had success has been there.

5. Choosing the right offer

The world of affiliate marketing is overflowing with offers and it is always difficult to choose the right one.

Do not make the mistake of trying to grab as many offers as possible and throw them all together in a cheesy way.

Start with one campaign at a time. Slowly and clearly.

Do not even waste too much time looking for the perfect campaign or the one that will make you the most money. Choose one and focus exclusively on that one, trying to optimize it as best you can.

<u>6. Don't be obsessed with learning.</u>

You never stop learning and the material you can find on the web is almost endless, so if you are trying to study as much as you can to get to the end of the tunnel, you have got it all wrong. It is okay to learn and get informed, in fact you need to, but without risking getting buried by too much information.

Overdosing on studying is not learning more, it is dying, and you'll soon find yourself discouraged and unmotivated. Focus on specific goals and start with those, getting right into the action. Act and start testing.

<u>Testing is the key word to succeed with affiliate marketing.</u>

There is always something to test and all the results of the tests you will have complied will be gold for the success of your affiliate business.

You can test traffic sources, offers, images, headlines, landing pages, colors, techniques, pricing, hosting etc. The difference between those who succeed and those who do not lies in testing and analyzing the results.

<u>7 Imitate and then innovate.</u>

One of the most effective techniques in affiliations is definitely this: look at what successful marketers do and try to imitate them, once you've succeeded, don't stop there, evolve their strategy. Try to do better. To be really successful, you have to innovate their idea, differentiate it, evolve it, even a little, but make it unique, only in this way success is guaranteed. Try to be always updated, because the market is constantly evolving, especially in the world of the web.

Try to always give 110% of yourself, put it all and you will see that you will always get great things. All that is left for me is to wish you a safe journey, good business, and good affiliate marketing!

This has been:

The Beginner's Guide to Affiliate Marketing: What the New Rich Teach Their Followers

The Seven Steps to Generate a Commission, How to Start from Scratch and Generate Organic Traffic

Written by Mike Armstrong

Copyright 2021 by Mike Armstrong

Production Copyright by Mike Armstrong